Seven Dimensions to Fulfilling Your Call

7 Seven Dimensions to Fulfilling Your Call

A Relentless Pursuit of God's Assignment For Your Life

KELVIN COLLINS

© 2015 by Kelvin Collins. All rights reserved.

Trusted Books is an imprint of Deep River Books. The views expressed or implied in this work are those of the author. To learn more about Deep River Books, go online to www.DeepRiverBooks.com.

No part of this publication may be reproduced, stored in a retrieval system, or transmitted in any way by any means—electronic, mechanical, photocopy, recording, or otherwise—without the prior permission of the copyright holder, except as provided by USA copyright law.

Scripture quotations marked NLT are taken from the *Holy Bible, New Living Translation*, copyright © 1996, 2004, 2007. Tyndale House Publishers Inc., Carol Stream, Illinois 60188. All rights reserved.

Scripture references marked NIV are taken from the *Holy Bible, New International Version*®, NIV®. Copyright © 1973, 1978, 1984 by Biblica, Inc.™ Used by permission of Zondervan. All rights reserved worldwide. www.zondervan.com

Scripture references marked NKJV are taken from the *New King James Version*. Copyright © 1982 by Thomas Nelson, Inc. All rights reserved.

Scripture references marked Wuest are taken from *The New Testament: An Expanded Translation* by Kenneth S. Wuest. © Copyright Wm. B. Eerdmans Publishing Co. 1961. All rights reserved.

Bible Soft References

(DOUAY-RHEIMS) HOLY BIBLE: DOUAY-RHEIMS TRANSLATION PC Study Bible formatted electronic database Copyright © 2006 by Biblesoft, Inc. All rights reserved.

(TLB) THE LIVING BIBLE Copyright © 1971. Used by permission of Tyndale House Publishers, Inc., Wheaton, IL 60189. All rights reserved.

(BBE) BIBLE IN BASIC ENGLISH PC Study Bible formatted electronic database Copyright © 2006 by Biblesoft, Inc. All rights reserved.

(RSV) REVISED STANDARD VERSION OF THE BIBLE, Copyright © 1946, 1952, 1971 by the Division of Christian Education of the National Council of the Churches of Christ in the USA, and is used by permission.

(HCSB) HOLMAN CHRISTIAN STANDARD BIBLE Copyright © 1999, 2000, 2002, 2003, 2005 by Holman Bible Publishers. All rights reserved.

(CJB) COMPLETE JEWISH BIBLE Copyright © 1998 by David H. Stern All rights reserved.

(AMP) AMPLIFIED BIBLE Copyright © 1954, 1958, 1962, 1964, 1965, 1987 by The Lockman Foundation, La Habra, CA 90631 All rights reserved. www.lockman.org

(ASV) The American Standard Version Electronic Database. Copyright © 1988, 2003, 2006 by Biblesoft, Inc. All rights reserved.

ISBN 13: 978-1-63269-040-1
Library of Congress Catalog Card Number: 2010904765

DEDICATION

This book is dedicated to my Lord and Savior Jesus Christ for it's His Call on my life that I'm fulfilling. To my dad, Manoah Collins Sr. who modeled for me what it means to be a man and to my mom, Willie Ruth Collins (1936-2005) who loved me unconditionally.

ACKNOWLEDGEMENTS

Words cannot express how much I love and appreciate my wife Angela. Thank you for all your love, encouragement and support. Thank you for believing in me and traveling this road with me. Our eyes have yet to see all that God has in store for us.

I appreciate my amazing children, Joshua, for his leadership, Keilah for her encouragement & creativity, and Elim, for his refreshing wisdom. I thank God for implanting you all into our lives.

I'm indebted to William Davis and Christine Davis (1931-2011), who I affectionately know as pop and mom. Thanks for not only being my father and mother in-law but a spiritual covering.

I am immensely grateful to Pastor's James and Marylyn Hill and the Northside Christian Center family who supported my family and I on many levels as God was cultivating the gifts in our lives. Northside Christian Center, Tulsa OK will always have a place in my heart.

I am so thankful for all those who encouraged, participated and supported Psalmsart Ministries throughout the years.

Thanks also to my writing coach, Lee Warren. Your input was invaluable. I'm especially appreciative to Mike Owens, Bill Carmichael, and the Deep River Books staff. Your timing was impeccable.

CONTENTS

Forward................................... vii
Introduction ix

The First Dimension: Consulting God
Chapter 1: The Call Has Definition................. 1
Chapter 2: The Purpose of the Call................ 15

The Second Dimension: Understanding Our Position in Christ
Chapter 3: Understanding Who You Are 31
Chapter 4: The Call Sets the Priority 49

The Third Dimension: The Right Pursuit
Chapter 5: What Did Jesus Pursue? 65
Chapter 6: What Did Paul Pursue?................ 79

The Fourth Dimension: Understanding Our Role
Chapter 7: The Call Defines Us................... 97
Chapter 8: Finding Our Place 116

The Fifth Dimension: Total Dependence Upon God's Grace

Chapter 9: The Call Defines How We Accomplish the Call 133

Chapter 10: Stewards of Our Gifts 151

The Sixth Dimension: Following God's Sovereign Will

Chapter 11: The Call Defines What We Are to Accomplish 173

Chapter 12: God Navigates Our Course 190

The Seventh Dimension: It's All About God's Timing

Chapter 13: Timing Is Critical to Success 207

Chapter 14: Proper Discernment 226

Appendix 1 241

Endnotes 243

FOREWORD

GROWING UP IN a spiritually charged environment mostly under my pastoral leadership and pursuing the educational and spiritual mandates to fulfil his call; Kelvin, after years of serving in various ministry capacities, felt inspired to set forth 7-Dimensions of fulfilling the call as revealed to him by the Holy Spirit.

Kelvin's devotion to God and his purpose driven life facilitated by his leadership involvement while serving in key roles in church ministry, has brought him to this juncture which has enabled him to release this message into the body of Christ.

The truths of God that he shares in the pages of this book will leave an indelible impression upon every reader who will reflect upon its contents and heed the admonition to respond to the call.

The author spares no pain in delineating how the call placed on your life is critical and binding. The course of your life and your eternal rewards hinge on its fulfillment.

He encourages us to breathe a sigh of relief and offers a way of release from any ambivalence and frustration regarding the call. He informs and assures one that God not only placed the call in us but also has deposited gifts, visions and anointings necessary for its fulfillment.

The author refers to this infusion of God's life and ability at work in us as a necessary ingredient in receiving a revelation of Jesus Christ and a proper understanding of our position in Christ. When you realize that your sufficiency is not based on human ability but on God's power and the forces of heaven which stands behind you, you become invincible.

Kelvin, step by step, takes us through his book using many illustrations and citing numerous life experiences and finally brings the reader to the point of revealing the purpose for the call and all that God has placed and entrusted in us. Without doubt, the contents of this book from cover to cover, is packed full of gems and nuggets to enlighten you, direct you, and inspire you to walk step-by-step with faith and confidence on the journey of fulfilling the call. Faith to see the mission accomplished before the journey begins is the goal and main objective of the author. You can now begin or continue your journey.

—Pastor James E. Hill
Northside Christian Center
Tulsa OK

INTRODUCTION

IN LISTENING TO the media, you will most likely agree that chaos is happening all around the world. Governments and leaders worldwide are struggling because they can't find real solutions to the myriad of problems our generation faces. Even though these problems attempt to paint a picture of hopelessness, the bible reminds us that there is hope for the world and as believers, God chose to make us a part of the solution. This hope lies within each of us.

In the midst of all the perplexities of the world, God has strategically placed the Church right in the center of all the action. The body of Christ is the catalyst of love, hope, and deliverance. We are the extended hands of the great physician Jesus Christ. Through us, the body of Christ, God is able to apply His healing balm of love to the world. The Church is God's voice.

The earth is waiting for the manifestation of the sons of God. We are co-laboring with the Holy Spirit and act as midwives to birth sons and daughters of God into His kingdom. We are joint laborers with God in establishing His Kingdom on earth until the final day when the kingdoms of this world become the kingdoms of our God.

The past and present have forged great leaders in the body of Christ who have paved the way toward Christ's return. As I watch to see who has the word for this hour to lead our generation, I realize that it's going to take more than those who appear on television or Internet, speak on the radio, and have mass distribution of books, DVDs and CDs to reach this generation. It will take all of us, including those who are currently unknown to the masses, but who are presently being forged by test and time. That means both you and I play a vital part in God's plan. Both heaven and earth are waiting for each of us to become who we're supposed to be and to achieve what we're supposed to do.

In Acts 13:22, God said He found David, a man who had His heart and who would do His will. Notice, first God found David. If God found him, it means He must have been looking for him. Also, there was something in David that caused God to look for him. What was it? It was David's willingness to allow God to use him.

Thankfully, God hasn't stopped looking for people like David. God's eyes run to and fro for that one whose heart is perfect toward Him. Why? So He can get His will accomplished through those who have a heart like David did. Are you the next one God is looking for?

Just as there are essential elements to building houses, there are indispensable components involved in building the lives of those on whom rests the call of God. Living without understanding could lead to pursuit of the wrong things and impede completing our God-given assignment on earth. If we don't take time to discover what God had in mind when He called us, we can limit the power of God in our lives.

INTRODUCTION

Too often we interpret the call of God in terms of accomplishments only. While it is true that God has called us to do a specific work, we must understand that sometimes we never get at God's real call because we refuse to go beyond the work. If God has called you to a television ministry to reach the masses with the gospel or even to build a place to provide jobs for the unemployed or to build soup kitchens to feed the homeless, you are performing noble feats. However, if you define the call of God in these terms only, then you are only focusing on what God wants done. Unfortunately, this perception will restrict your faith from believing God for the impossibilities that have already been prearranged for you.

Another way we potentially limit ourselves is by characterizing our call only in terms of a vocation. Some are called to the five-fold ministry as a pastor or evangelist. For others, their calling may be to become a doctor or even an author. However, to define your call only in terms of a vocation would be equivalent to viewing all that God has in store for you through a keyhole, which consequently creates a narrow view. Simply put, your vocation is not conclusive of your call; it's a means to the end but not the end itself.

One of the things I learned while writing this book is that the call of God is not a mystery. It's not something on its way to you, it's already here, and it's in you. If you haven't discovered it, it's just a matter of time before you will. The process of discovering the fullness of the call is like an archeological journey. Just as an archeologist needs special tools, God gives us the utensils we need to begin our own excavation process of discovering who we are and what He's called us to do.

God made the call on your life so vast and multifaceted. It's designed so that you can make a positive impact in this earth and for the kingdom of God. Its ripple effects are to impact your generation and generations to come, and yet its design is simple enough for you to carry out through effortless obedience.

This book is a tool to help you on this spiritual journey to uncovering the seven dimensions related to your call. My prayer is that as you dig into the nuggets of truth in this book, the Holy Spirit will enlarge your perspective of the call and intensify your desire to seek Him and to pursue His heart concerning your call. After all, when it is all said and done and we stand before God, we all want to hear Him say, "Well Done. You fulfilled the call on your life. Enter into the Joy of the Lord." Now, let's begin our study of the "Seven Dimensions to Fulfilling Your Call" by first defining what it means to be called.

THE FIRST DIMENSION: CONSULTING GOD

CHAPTER 1

THE CALL HAS DEFINITION

> Who has saved us and called us with a holy calling, not according to our works, but according to His own purpose and grace which was given to us in Christ Jesus before time began ... to which I was appointed a preacher, an apostle, and a teacher of the Gentiles.
> —2 Timothy 1:9, 11, NKJV

MAX LUCADO WROTE an inspiring children's book called *You Are Special*, which was later made into a children's video.[1] The story takes place in a village called Wemmicksville. The village was filled with little wooden people called Wemmicks, each hand carved by their creator named Eli. These Wemmicks spent their waking hours exchanging stickers—a star or a gray dot. This exchange was based on their perception of each other. A star signified they did something worthy of it; a gray dot represented someone who didn't fit in, someone who didn't measure up, or something done that was undesirable by the Wemmick's standards.

7 DIMENSIONS TO FULFILLING YOUR CALL

The main character was a wooden boy named Punchinello. He was covered in gray stickers because he was perceived as incompetent and lacking talent. Other Wemmicks, including the mayor, treated him and others like him as outcasts of society. Punchinello tried to earn a star, but it didn't matter what he did, he didn't measure up.

One day, Punchinello ran across another Wemmick named Lucia. He noticed something different about her. She didn't have any gray dots or stars. Not one sticker would stick to her little, wooden body. This caught Punchinello's attention. She was different from all the others, and Punchinello discovered that it was because she had had an encounter with Eli, their creator.

Punchinello finally met Eli for himself and learned a powerful lesson. He asked Eli why stickers didn't stick to Lucia. Eli told him, "Because she has decided that what I think is more important than what they think."[2] Like Lucia, Punchinello began spending more time with Eli. As he did, he began to understand Eli's unconditional love for him and was less concerned about how the other Wemmicks perceived him. After this, the stickers would no longer stick to Punchinello.

This story is an allegory of how God sees us as His creation. What's interesting is that in order for Punchinello to really understand his value, he had to consult Eli, his creator. When he did, those consultations changed his focus and clarified his purpose.

To fully understand the purpose for the call on our lives and what it encompasses, we have to consult our Creator—God—which represents the First Dimension of the Call. The call on our lives has definition and a final outcome. Only God can define it for us. Only He can clarify His intent for each of us. We can focus on what matters when we take on the view of our Creator.

THE CALL HAS DEFINITION

Summoned by a Heavenly Court

It was a bright sunny afternoon, and I was on my way back to work after lunch. It was my day to fast, and I had just had a wonderful time of devotions. I was excited because I had made time for God. I was in my own world. Suddenly, I realized that I was hearing a sound, as if someone in my ear was calling my name out of a deep sleep.

I looked up into my rearview mirror and noticed a dark brown car behind me, nothing special. It looked like something a coworker would drive, but this car definitely made a statement with its blue lights flashing through the window.

Where did that come from? I thought. It was like the car had been shrouded in a cloaking device, and then suddenly, it had materialized. I pulled over.

She stepped out of the car all suited up like a knight in King Arthur's court ready to joust. At least that's what was reflected in her demeanor, although the lance was actually her badge and her gun.

"Sir, do you know why I pulled you over?" The officer asked.

"No," I responded.

"Didn't you see that sign that says, 'No left turn?'"

"No ma'am, I never saw any sign. What sign?" I responded, surprised.

By her look, I knew my response didn't faze her a bit. But I really didn't see any sign. All I did was exit off the interstate, and when I got to the yield sign, instead of merging to the right since there was no traffic, I took the liberty of turning left—kind of a half U-turn—and went the opposite direction. It looked OK to me.

"Sir, it's illegal to make a left from this point," she insisted.

"Ah, sorry officer, I won't let it happen again," I replied. "I really didn't see a sign."

By the look on her face, I might as well have been speaking a foreign language. She wasn't hearing it.

"Driver's license and registration please!" she responded sternly. I had my driver's license ready, but I had to reach for my registration.

"It's in my glove box," I said cautiously. It was one thing for me to be nervous, but I definitely wasn't going to reach too fast and make the officer nervous.

She walked back to her vehicle. After a few minutes, she returned.

"Here ya go, have a nice day," she said as she handed me a yellow sheet of paper. *Great, it's just a warning*, I thought until I took a closer look. It was a citation. The ticket stated, "You are summoned to appear in the general district court." That statement was followed by the court date.

I noticed the details used the word "summons," which meant I'd received a command by an authority of the state in the form of a traffic citation to appear in court. Failure to show up or make some kind of amends could lead to disciplinary actions, including, monetary fines, suspension of my driver's license, and more.

In First Timothy 1:9, the apostle Paul states that both he and Timothy have a call on their lives, and God called them with a "holy calling." The word "called" means to command or summon. Summon means to call forth, to demand the presence of.[3] Paul asserts that the Creator of heaven and earth issued a command regarding them. His apostleship and Timothy's pastorate were not a random events. God summoned them based on something He had on His mind.

Like Paul and Timothy, a Sovereign God has summoned us. This directive is more significant than a traffic citation, and it's dual fold. First, God summoned us into fellowship with His Son. It's our call into the kingdom to be separate from the world (see First Corinthians 1:9).

This means that God Almighty summoned you before the foundations of the earth. So, what should be your answer? "God I can't or God I won't?" Or is your answer, "God, I hear your voice, and I obey?" Unfortunately, just as one may choose to ignore a court order and suffer penalties, a person can choose not to heed God's call unto salvation and suffer the consequence which is much worse than a suspended license.

Secondly, God summoned us for service within His Kingdom. We are ambassadors for Christ in the earth. Jesus gave us the message of reconciliation and commanded us to go throughout the entire world and proclaim the gospel of the Kingdom. Also, God requires every believer to be equipped to do ministry (Ephesians 4:7–11). When you accepted God's invitation into His kingdom, you also accepted His summons into service.

Fundamentals of the Call

The call is tied to God's purpose for your life. Purpose relates to God's plan. The call is the command to be something and to complete something based on this purpose. So purpose is God's plan for your life, and the call is God's command over your life. Now let's explore six fundamental truths about the call.

1. God alone does the calling. Second Timothy 1:9 tells us that God calls us according to His private purpose. This call is so intricate that God alone reserved the right to call us. This means that we cannot call ourselves, and no one on earth can place a call on our life. It was, "... given to us in Christ Jesus before time began."

2. We cannot choose what our call is. God created us with the power to choose, however, this is one area where we don't have a choice in the matter. In his book, *The Purpose Driven Life*, Rick Warren comments that we can choose a lot of things in life: our car, our clothes, or what we will eat for dinner, but we can't choose our purpose in life.[4] The same holds true about the call.

   Furthermore, neither our parents, nor our pastor, nor our boss can choose what our call is. God may use your parent or others to affirm what He established, but keep in mind, our Sovereign God determined our call before our parents were even born, before the church existed, and even before our boss ever found his or her first minimum wage job. The decision was made before creation.
3. Disobeying the call of God is not an option. The Old Testament prophet Jonah knew God had called him to go to Nineveh and yet ran in the opposite direction. Consequently, Jonah found himself in a predicament that he couldn't solve—in the belly of a huge fish. Had Jonah been obedient, he could have avoided such difficulty. Jonah's experience teaches us that if we choose not to follow God's call, we might find ourselves in the belly of life's hardships. Our will does not determine God's will *for* our life, but our will does determine God's will *in* our life.
4. God qualified us for our call. If we don't have a seminary degree, does that mean God can't call us to preach? On the contrary, we don't need a degree in higher education for God to qualify us for our calling. We are qualified for the call because God chose us.

THE CALL HAS DEFINITION

God called Gideon to deliver the children of Israel out of the hands of the Midianites (see Judges 6). Gideon's excuses to God were that he was afraid, poor, and the least in his father's house. In other words, he felt he wasn't qualified to lead because of low self-esteem, his economic situation, and family background. But God still used him because he was available and obedient. We cannot allow our past, background, or feelings about ourselves to hinder us from pursuing our call when we know God has chosen us. God qualifies us, not our background.

Moreover, heaven's decisive factor is not based on man's criterion. In First Samuel 16, God sent the prophet Samuel to Jesse's house to anoint Israel's next king among Jesse's sons. Samuel's first choice was David's oldest brother, Eliab. But God refused him and told the prophet he used the wrong criteria. Samuel's benchmarks were based on external factors. God, however, looks at our heart and sees our potential.

5. We can't fulfill our call alone. The idea that one doesn't need others to fulfill our call is incorrect. God uses people to help us to get where He wants us to go. God puts key people in our lives to help release the visions, gifts, and callings in our lives. Jethro mentored Moses. Elijah was a father to Elisha. God used Potipher, Joseph's employer, to develop and release his gifts. God used David's friendship with Jonathan as a source of encouragement and protection. God uses people to affirm and release the call in our lives.

The Power of What God Said

This leads to the sixth fundamental truth about our call: Our call is based on what God already said. Independence Day in the United States illustrates this principle. Annually, on July 4th, the United States of America celebrates its independence from Great Britain. The day commemorates the ratification of a famous document called The Declaration of Independence, authored by Thomas Jefferson, which emphasizes the respect, equality, protection, and liberty for all the nation's citizens.

To date, this perpetual document still serves as the foundation for the nation's moral standards and political philosophies. This document continues to influence the nation's laws and other national decisions, even though it was established over 200 years ago.

God's Word is an even more perpetual document than The Declaration of Independence. God made His declarations eons ago that still effect mankind today because God is committed to what He said.

To really understand the value of what God has already spoken, we must understand two things. First, God doesn't change. God doesn't even cast a shadow when He's turning (James 1:17). He's the eternal God (Deuteronomy 33:27). Further, Hebrews 13:8 declares that Jesus Christ is the same yesterday, today, and forever. Yesterday represents from a second ago back to eternities past. Today represents the present or now. Tomorrow represents the next second into future millenniums. Again, Jesus Christ is the same right now, as He was a second ago to eternities past, as He will be in the next second into the future millenniums. God never changes.

Second, God's Word is settled forever; this means God's Word is unmovable (Psalm 119:89). When God speaks

THE CALL HAS DEFINITION

something, it's established. Therefore, what God said yesterday still holds true today. Let's look at how creation follows the two principles above.

God created the universe by speaking it into existence. Scientists have confirmed that the universe is still expanding. Not only is it expanding, but it is doing so at an accelerated rate. In fact, some astronomers thought that this expansion was slowing down but have concluded that "some mysterious force was acting against the pull of gravity, shoving galaxies away from each other at ever-increasing speeds."[5]

Psalm 33:6 explains this phenomenon stating, "The LORD merely spoke, and the heavens were created. He breathed the word, and all the stars were born."[6] God spoke this universe into existence, and to this day, it's still expanding because of what God said billions of years ago.

God created the earth by command. Today, the earth rotates on its axis because it's being held together "by the mighty power of his command."[7] Additionally, God commanded the earth to produce vegetation and fruit. According to Genesis 1:11, "Then God said, 'Let the land produce vegetation: seed-bearing plants and trees on the land that bear fruit with seed in it, according to their various kinds.' And it was so."[8] To this day, trees and vegetation continue to produce fruit, thus obeying the Creator.

Finally, in Genesis 1:9, God commanded the waters on earth to gather in one place so there would be dry land. And in Proverbs 8:29, He commanded the waters to stay within their borders. To this day, even when there are floods and tsunamis, the oceans and seas cannot permanently supersede their boundaries.

So if the universe, the earth, nature, and water are still obeying God today because of something He already said, then what about you and me? The call on our lives is based on the same principles: God issued a command about us yesterday, and it still stands today because God does not change (Malachi 3:6). God's word is filled with so much authority and power that what He said yesterday (eternities past) is still creating our tomorrows (future millenniums).

God is not making things up as we go along. He doesn't wake up, reaching for His morning coffee and trying to plan our day, nor do our life events take Him by surprise. Everything we experience may not be His divine will, but thank God that according to Romans 8:28, "All things work together for the good of those who love God: those who are called according to His purpose,"[9] In spite of life's oppositions, setbacks, or our own mistakes, God is still in control and working all things in our favor. So why is what God already said about us so important? Because the call on our lives is directly interrelated to what He has spoken.

A Finished Perspective

Sometimes we make the mistake of considering what God is saying to us today as something God is going to do rather than as something He has already done. When God makes a promise today, it's already fulfilled because God speaks from what I call a "finished perspective." When we discover the calling on our life, i.e. the call to missions, to pastor, to the medical or education field, etc., and come to realize how God is directing our steps, it may seem like just the beginning, but from God's viewpoint, it's already done. When God speaks to us pertaining to our call, we have to grasp it as if it was yesterday's news. If we don't, we can become vulnerable to doubt and unbelief, which impedes the faith we need, to fulfill the call.

What is faith? It is the confident assurance that something we want is going to happen. It is the certainty that

THE CALL HAS DEFINITION

what we hope for is waiting for us, even though we cannot see it up ahead (see Hebrews 11:1, TLB).

According to Hebrews 11, faith is now. It's "the confident assurance that something we want is going to happen." You can anchor your faith on God's Word to you today because what He promised was actually done yesterday. Abraham's calling was based on this same principle. God called Abraham to be the Father of many nations before Abraham was even born. Abraham had to fulfill what God already said. Consider the following verses pertaining to Abraham's call:

> Now the LORD had said to Abram: "Get out of your country, from your family and from your father's house, to a land that I will show you. I will make you a great nation; I will bless you and make your name great; and you shall be a blessing."
> —Genesis 12:1–2 NKJV

> (As it is written, "I have made you a father of many nations") in the presence of Him whom he believed—God, who gives life to the dead and calls those things which do not exist as though they did.
> —Romans 4:17 NKJV

According to Genesis 12, Abraham's previous name was Abram, which meant "high father," and Sarah's name was Sarai meaning "my princess." When God spoke into Abram's "today," Abram heard it and perceived it as something God would do in the future. Because of this limited perspective, his faith could not fully latch onto God's Word. Consequently, Abram viewed God's promise as futuristic, so it gave room for the negative circumstances surrounding him to outweigh what God was saying to him. I can imagine Abram thought, "Doesn't God see my circumstances?" His wife couldn't bear children, and they both were getting older. Doubt caused him to look for an alternative solution, like expecting God to use a relative or to use Hagar, his maidservant, instead of Sarai to have a child.

A finished perspective considers the end at the beginning. According to Isaiah 46:10, "At the beginning I announce the end, proclaim in advance things not yet done; and I say that my plan will hold, I will do everything I please to do."[10] God speaks nothing contrary to what He Himself already established.

Calling for Destiny

Our beginning is equivalent to what Romans 4 calls "things that do not exist." From Abrams's perspective, the call to become the father of a multitude did not exist. For him, he was about to embark on a new beginning. However, when God spoke into Abram's "today," He spoke with the end in mind. In God's eyes, Abram was already the father of many nations (a finished perceptive), but how could He convince Abram to see himself from this perspective? The father of many nations had never existed on Abram's level before. God had a solution to get Abram to agree with Him and to change what Abram was saying about himself. This way, Abram's faith could see the beginning as the end and not as the beginning. To accomplish this, God changed his name from Abram (high father) to Abraham which means "father of a multitude," to reflect what He had already said.

An echo was created in Abraham's ears when God changed his name. Webster defines a human echo as one who closely imitates or repeats another's words, ideas, or acts,[11] so every time Abraham heard his name, or when he introduced himself, he and others were literally echoing what God said. These words were agreeing with God as they were spoken from a finished perspective.

God knew that if Abraham heard the echo enough, he actually would start believing it. Abraham was repeating God's Word, God's idea that eventually caused him to act God's way. This process caused his faith to elevate to where it needed to be. Eventually his faith caused what did not exist to come into being. His wife experienced the same miracle, because God changed her name from Sarai to Sarah, from my princess to princess of all families of the earth.

When God speaks to you today about your calling, that word is literally an echo of something He has already said. Just like Abraham's call was already established eternities ago, so was ours. Understanding this concept provides hope and peace to the struggles challenging us.

Since the call on our lives is merely an echo of what God has already said, it's easier to take hold of it by faith, especially if we're willing to repeat and believe the echo of God's Word. Repeating what God said, positions us to be in agreement with God. This agreement alone will enable us to experience all that God released within our calls. We'll walk into everything God foreordained. If you believe and keep saying what God says about your call, even if it doesn't exist, your "today" can be transformed by the eternal reality of what God has already said about you. This truth implores us to consult God to find out what He had in mind when He called us, since He called us "according to His own private purpose."

Chapter 1

7 Principles

1. When you accepted God's invitation into His kingdom, you also accepted His summons into service.

2. Purpose relates to God's plan, while the call is the command to be something and to complete something based on this purpose.

3. Your will does not determine God's will *for* your life; but your will does determine God's will *in* your life

4. You are qualified for the call because God chose you. God qualifies you, not your background.

5. God issued a command about us yesterday, and it still stands today because God does not change.

6. When God makes a promise today, it's already fulfilled because God speaks from a "finished perspective."

7. When God speaks to you today about your calling, you are literally hearing an echo of something He already said.

CHAPTER 2

THE PURPOSE OF THE CALL

> And we know that all things work together for good to them that love God, to them who are the called according to his purpose.
> —Romans 8:28 KJV

YEARS AGO, I worked for a particular company in the IT department. We had a goal of transforming our computer help desk into a world-class call center. Our help desk was in its infancy stages, and a lot of processes and procedures were still undefined. One day my boss challenged my colleagues and me with writing a mission statement for our new call center.

So off we went like writers, scratching our heads, mentally hammering, determined to create our mission statement. After we struggled for a while, my boss made a simple statement, "How can you truly define your mission if you don't know the vision of the company? Your mission statement must align with the vision of the corporate office."

So we stepped back and took time to review the vision and goals of our corporate office. Afterward, we felt as if a light bulb was turned on. We had more insight, were able to apply our energies, and created our new mission statement toward achieving what we envisioned as a world-class call center, all in view of the corporate vision.

This applies to God's call on our lives, for without vision, how can we identify our mission? To identify with the call on our lives, we must first become familiar with heaven's vision. This will give our mission a sense of purpose.

Master Design

When building a house, the first stage of the building process is to obtain an architectural blueprint. A blueprint outlines the big picture. It's the master design. It's the vision laid out in detail of what the house is supposed to look like when the construction project is completed.

God has a master design that authenticates why He can declare the end from the beginning (see Isaiah 46:10). His master design was fashioned out of the counsel of His will (see Ephesians 1:10) and determined the purpose for why He called us. It also outlines all the details. It's the big picture. John Maxwell, author of, *How Successful People Think*, says, "To get things done, you need focus. However, to get the right things done, you also need to consider the big picture. Only by putting your daily activities in context of the big picture will you be able to stay on target."[1]

In order to grasp how our call supports God's master design, we must first understand the big picture—heaven's vision. Accomplishing this demands that we satisfy this First Dimension of the Call—Consulting God.

To help gain a perspective, let's look at why God called the prophet Jeremiah. What was the purpose for the prophetic anointing on Jeremiah's life? If we understand why Jeremiah was called, we'll gain insight into God's design for his ministry (see Jeremiah 1:5).

Jeremiah was God's mouthpiece for the nation of Israel who were God's chosen people. Israel's calling was to reach all nations of the earth for God's glory, however, Israel rejected God. Because of the hardness of their hearts, they fell into God's judgment, were evicted from their land, and sent into Babylonian exile. God called Jeremiah as a prophetic voice to Israel to proclaim repentance and hope to them. The call on Jeremiah's life had a purpose. He was not called for himself but for something greater. He was called to influence a nation. Likewise, a divine purpose drives the calling on our lives.

Life's Choices

One Christmas afternoon while my wife and I were preparing dinner, my youngest son (who was elementary aged at the time) and teenage daughter were playing the board game, "The Game of Life," by Milton Bradley. The game simulates a person's life journey from a career or college to retirement. Both kids ran to me in a playful panic after finishing the game.

"Dad!" my son hollered. "When I passed the spot to get married, I had to get married whether I wanted to or not. Then I landed on the spot marked 'You got a baby girl!' Then later on in the game, I landed on 'You got Twins,'" he continued.

His sister hadn't landed on either of the spaces about having children, and he was really stressing out.

My son continued to express, "In the game, I didn't want to get married or anything, but I ended up retiring from a career of being a summer teacher with a wife, three kids, and no money! You know what made me lose the game?" he asked. "I had to pay taxes! It was so wrong! My sister had the life I wanted, and I had the life she wanted."

Then it was my daughter's turn. By this time, she was playfully upset.

"Dad," she said. "In the game, I went from being an artist, to being an entertainer, to finally retiring as a computer consultant. All I wanted was children, but I ended up retiring rich with no kids! Dad, I know I chose the college route and was successful, but by the end of the game, I realized it wasn't the life I wanted."

Thank God that conversation was just about a game. It was interesting to hear how my kids felt about their life's journey, although lived through a board game. What's more interesting is that we, as adults, at times, find ourselves feeling the same way, dissatisfied with our life choices. In his book, *Understanding the Purpose & Power of Men*, Myles Munroe states, "If you don't know why you were born, you could live a completely wrong life."[2] Similarly, if you don't understand why you're called, you could be serving God in church or ministry for all the wrong reasons.

Running Your Course

Hebrews 12:1 speaks of us running a race. To contrast, pursuing our call is like running a marathon. A runner's goal is to finish the race to win a prize, but what if he or she is unsure of where the finish line is or what the prize is? What if the runner doesn't even know whether he or she is even in the correct race? How would that affect the runner's ability to win?

For some, relating to the call is the same. Does it make sense not to know what the goal is, where you're going, or even why you're running? It's not enough just to know you're an incredible runner? It's just as important to know if you're in the right race, running to obtain the correct prize for you.

Paul considered himself to be running in a race. In 1 Corinthians 9:24, he tells us to run that we may obtain. Paul knew why he was running and what the goal was. In Philippians 3:14, he says, "I press toward the mark for the prize." He understood the reward for achieving the goal, and he finished his course (see 2 Timothy 4:7).

The kingdom of God needs you, so how does what you're doing fit into God's master plan? You need to know why you're running. Without this understanding, you may be running in vain or running to obtain the wrong thing. The first step in fulfilling your call is realizing God's purpose for calling you. Your call is directly connected to the big picture—the Heavenly vision. For that reason, let's start with before time began.

Vision from the Beginning

What is it about man that has God's full attention? Why do we occupy His heart? It's because humanity is the Father's beloved above all creation (see Psalm 8:4). He yearned to communicate with His sons and daughters and to spend eternities sharing the wealth of His love, glory, and grace. God prepared this earth with infinite resources of wealth to meet any and every need that mankind would ever have.

To achieve His desire, God began to write a plan. The Father was the first Author the universe has ever known. He wrote volumes of pages designing His will for His humanity. Now come with me as we review the first chapter of His plan.

Creation

> He is the image of the invisible God, the firstborn over all creation. For by Him all things were created that are

in heaven and that are on earth, visible and invisible, whether thrones or dominions or principalities or powers. All things were created through Him and for Him. And He is before all things, and in Him all things consist.
—Colossians 1:15–17 NKJV

Before anything ever existed, God existed—the Father, the Son, and the Holy Spirit (see Genesis 1:1–2; John 1:1–3). God and His heavenly counsel determined to maintain order that all creation would originate out of one source. Therefore, the sovereignty of God determined that Christ, the Word, would be the source for anything created in heaven, in earth, and even under the earth (see Colossians 1:16, Ephesians 3:9, and Hebrews 1:2–10). Christ was made the firstborn over all creation.

1. As the firstborn, Christ existed before there was anything.
2. As the firstborn, Christ is the originator. All things were created by the Word.
3. As the firstborn, Christ is the source of all life. Life gets its breath from the Word. The Word ignites the spirit of every human being that comes into the world. The Word gives life and energy to everything called into being. He holds everything together (Hebrews 1:3; 11:3). The *Adam Clarke Commentary* explains:

> As every effect depends upon its cause, and cannot exist without it; so creation, which is an effect of the power and skill of the Creator, can only exist and be preserved by a continuance of that energy that first gave it being.[3]

4. As the firstborn, Christ is head over everything created. All creation finds itself under His domain. Through Christ, the apex of authority, the creative power of God flowed in divine order, establishing harmony in creation.

Delegation Once

It is here that we turn to the next chapter in God's book—Delegation. As the pages turn, we see the creation of man. In Genesis 1:26, God said, "Let Us make man in Our image, according to Our likeness; let them have dominion over the fish of the sea, over the birds of the air, and over the cattle, over all the earth and over every creeping thing that creeps on the earth."[4] Man was made in God's image and likeness, and his name was Adam.

God determined that Adam would rule and dominate the earth, so He passed on the authority of the earth to him. Similar to a power of attorney agreement, Adam had the legal right to act on behalf of His Creator. Through Adam, God maintained order in the earth, but this authority came with responsibility and the criterion was obedience (Gen. 2:5, 15–17).

The Disarrangement

Later chapters in God's plan reflected how chaos took place. As the pages turn, we see Adam forfeiting this authority by conferring with God's enemy Lucifer, aka Satan, the fallen archangel. Anarchy began with Lucifer being evicted from heaven when he attempted to usurp God's throne. This disarray culminated with the fall of man through Lucifer's deception and Adam's transgression (see Genesis 3:1–6).

Everything God entrusted to man, Adam willingly gave over to Lucifer. These two chaotic events left heaven with a vacancy and the earth in pandemonium. Sin was birthed, and now the earth groaned and travailed as it was made subject to frustration and corruption. Sin created a barrier between God and man. At birth, the human race is shaped in iniquity through sin's parturition canal and distant from God because of the severed relationship.

According to Isaiah 49:15, God asked a question, "Can a woman forget her infant, so as not to have pity on the son of her womb? and if she should forget, yet will not I forget thee."[5]

As a mother longs for her child, God longed for His children and determined beforehand that He would not let His creation pass into the enemy's hands without a fight. God desired that we would return back to Him and become what He intended for us to be. Therefore, God turned to the next chapter in His book. This chapter uncovers the mystery that was concealed until the appropriate time. The mystery is called Redemption (see Ephesians 3:9; 1 Corinthians 2:7–8). Now we are at the final chapters of God's plan

The Mystery Unfolds

> And he saw that there was no man, and wondered that there was no intercessor: therefore his arm brought salvation unto him; and his righteousness, it sustained him.
> —Isaiah 59:16 KJV

God sought for one who could stand in the gap as an intercessor for all mankind, but there was none, so God sent His Son (see Philippians 2:5–11; 1 John 3:8b). The seam of the Father's plan was woven through the intervention of Christ. John 3:16 declares, "For God so loved the world that He gave His only begotten Son, that whoever believes in Him should not perish but have everlasting life."[6] Jesus Christ was the channel by which God's ultimate plan could be achieved. Jesus conquered Satan, took back man's authority, and then released the call to us to fulfill the Heavenly vision.

The Heavenly Vision

> He purposed in himself, with respect to an administration of the completion of the epochs of time to bring again to their original state all things in the Christ, the things in the heavens and the things in the earth.
> —Ephesians 1:10, Kenneth W. Wuest Translation

This verse explains God's Heavenly vision which is to reconcile all things in the heavens and in the earth back to its original state under the authority of Christ (see Colossians 1:20). It is for the purpose of bringing everything back to the authority of Christ that God has called us to support the vision of reconciliation. We are called to jointly participate in God's plan. Through us, God wants to establish His kingdom in the earth. The finish line is more than just making it to heaven. God wants to restore His authority and establish His kingdom in every arena of our lives, and we have a divine mandate to help achieve this purpose. Jesus taught us not only to pray that His kingdom come and His will be done but also, to actively participate in making it happen.

God is able to accomplish His vision of reckoning all things back under the authority of Christ by infusing three essential ingredients into our call.

1. **To Reconcile the World**

According to Second Corinthians 5:18–21, God was present in Christ reconciling the world back to Himself, and Christ has given each of us "the ministry of reconciliation."

The call on our lives compels us to go after the lost. Luke 15:4 gives us an example of the shepherd who left his ninety-nine sheep to find one lost sheep. That's how God feels about the lost. He loves them. The call on our lives invokes us to engage and be persistent in reaching the lost. In fact, those who reach the lost are a sparkle in God's eyes. Daniel 12:3 tell us, "Those who are wise will shine like the bright expanse of the heavens, and those who lead many to righteousness, like the stars forever and ever."[7]

2. **To Build the Body of Christ**

Intertwined within our call is the undeniable drive to build up the body of Christ. The body should grow in numbers and maturity. We are to help one another grow. When there is unity, there can be maturity. When God's love is properly distributed through each of us, then the body of Christ flourishes (see Ephesians 4:10–16).

3. **To Restore God's Glory**

God's wants His glory restored in humanity. To understand this, we must go back to how God extended His kingdom through Adam in the earth.

> What is man that You are mindful of him, And the son of man that You visit him? For You have made him a little lower than the angels, And You have crowned him with glory and honor. You have made him to have dominion over the works of Your hands; You have put all things under his feet.
> —Psalm 8:4–6 NKJV

First, Adam was a reflection of God, a container for God's glory. The glory of God is both the manifestation of what He has and what He is.[8] God's glory was Adam's

THE PURPOSE OF THE CALL

spiritual apparel; it clothed him inwardly and adorned him outwardly. He was crowned with glory and honor. Crown means to be encircled. God's glory surrounded Adam to the point that it covered him emotionally, spiritually, and physically. The glory was his protection, and nothing was exposed.

Glory means heavyweight and splendor. It also means copiousness, which is defined as yielding something in abundance; something present in large quantity.[9] What was present in Adam in such abundance was God's presence. The weightiness of God's presence flooded Adam's entire being. No other creature or any part of God's creation could house the presence of God, only man was created with that capacity.

As God's container of glory, Adam mirrored God's presence in the earth. He manifested all the virtues of his Creator. This glory was tangible. Nature could feel God when Adam was around. It experienced God's characteristics in a tangible way.

Secondly, Adam represented God's glory by exercising God's authority. To represent means to act on behalf of another, with all the rights and privileges of the one for whom you're standing in.[10] Adam stood in for God on earth to maintain God's authority.

Finally, Adam manifested God's glory by carrying out his work. God's glory was revealed through Adam's wisdom to name every animal, insect, plant, and every living creature in the earth. God's glory was visible as Adam applied God's wisdom in laboring in the garden.

Unfortunately, when Adam sinned, he ceased to be a perfect resemblance of God. He was now marred by sin. He ceased to yield God's presence in abundance when the act of sin severed him from the source of life. He lost his authority to rule the earth. No longer could he reflect, represent, or manifest God's glory.

God wants His glory restored in the earth. God sent Jesus, the second Adam, to restore what the first Adam lost. As part of the heavenly vision, God wants each of us to reflect, represent, and manifest His glory in the earth as Adam once did (see Romans 8:29–30).

God designed His plan, and after creation, He rested (see Genesis 2:2–3). Jesus fulfilled His call and is now sitting on the right hand of the Father (see Ephesians 1:20). Jesus knew that He had only three and a half years to finish an eternity's worth of work. It was through Christ that God's plan now progressed to its final chapter. Jesus entrusted the completion of the Father's plan to us, the body of Christ. We must finish what the call on Jesus' life started, because when time has reached its full maturity, and God closes this chapter of the book, Christ will return.

Therefore, the first step to fulfilling the call on our lives is to comprehend the heavenly vision. Now that we have insight into the purpose for the call, let's move forward to the Second Dimension of the Call which is Understand our Position in Christ.

Chapter 2

7 Principles

1. If you don't understand why you're called, you could be serving God in church or ministry for all the wrong reasons.

2. The kingdom of God needs you. So how does what you're doing fit into God's master plan?

3. God wants to restore His authority and establish His kingdom in every arena of our lives.

4. Jesus taught us not only to pray that His kingdom would come, and His will would be done but also, to actively participate in making it happen.

5. Christ fulfilled His mission and then released to us the call to fulfill the Heavenly vision.

6. As part of the heavenly vision, God wants each of us to reflect, represent, and manifest His glory in the earth.

7. We must finish what the call on Jesus' life started, because when time has reached its full maturity, and God closes this chapter of the book, Christ will return.

# THE SECOND DIMENSION: UNDERSTANDING OUR POSITION IN CHRIST

CHAPTER 3

UNDERSTANDING WHO YOU ARE

When Jesus came into the region of Caesarea Philippi, He asked His disciples, saying, "Who do men say that I, the Son of Man, am?"
—Matthew 16:13 NKJV

ONE DAY I had the opportunity to meet up with an old friend of my family. It had been 20 years since I saw him last. As we greeted each other, almost immediately, he broke down into tears and began to express his heart. He was overwhelmed with sadness concerning a family member of his who was a pastor. This pastor had been in the ministry for many years and, at some juncture in his life, had left the ministry and his family for a life of infidelity with another woman. The old friend continued to mournfully express how this pastor felt that God, family, and congregation were all to blame for the choices he made.

It is so easy to lose sight of who we are in the light of the Word, whenever we allow our hearts to be diverted from Christ Jesus as our focal point. This diversion enables the desires of the flesh to become accelerated and to position one right in the middle of a danger zone, and if not corrected, can lead one toward spiritual decline. This next dimension, Understanding Our Position in Christ, can help us avoid the risk of falling into at least three other dangerous pitfalls.

1. **Unhealthy Achievements.** Gordon MacDonald, leadership editor-at-large for *Christianity Today*, talks about the danger of Christian leaders losing touch with who they are in his article "Leader's Insight: When Leaders Implode." He comments: "It seems to me that when people become leaders of outsized organizations and movements, when they become famous and their opinions are constantly sought by the media, we ought to begin to become cautious. The very drive that propels some leaders toward extraordinary levels of achievement is a drive that often keeps expanding even after reasonable goals and objectives have been achieved. Like a river that breaks its levy that drive often strays into areas of excitement and risk that can be dangerous and destructive. Sometimes the drive appears to be unstoppable."[1]

2. **Emotional Fatigue.** In the article, "Survival Skills," pastor James Emery White speaks of guarding ones self against the danger of emotional depletion. He comments, "When you hurt, if you don't find something God-honoring to fill your tanks with, you'll find something that isn't God honoring. Or at the very least, you'll be vulnerable to something that isn't."[2]

3. **Spiritual Burnout.** This particular pastor's pursuit of his mission and the gift of shepherding and

neglecting this dimension of the calling, put him at risk of spiritual burnout. One of the signs of burnout is when what should be a joy becomes drudgery. You feel like your divine calling has become a weighted task. If we're not careful, we can fall into the trap, interpreting serving God as putting God first. Serving God is a critical part of our calling, however, we can allow that service to make us like Martha in Luke 10:38–42. She was so busy doing things *for* God that she wasn't doing enough *with* Him. Sometimes we make the same mistake. Again, making our service to God as our number one priority doesn't mean we've made God our number one priority.

Many in the body of Christ experience these unfortunate outcomes everyday. For the pastor in our present discussion, infidelity was the result. For others, the outcomes may vary, but the root of the problem is the same—losing sight of who we are. When we're mission-minded only, we set ourselves up to fail at reaching all that God has in store for us.

In the 1988 Summer Olympics a sprinter from Canada, set a world record running the 100-meter race. He won the gold medal and had anticipated going back to his country to celebrate his victory. However, disappointing news came when later he was disqualified for using a drug designed to boost his athletic performance.[3] Unfortunately, it didn't matter how much time, effort, planning, and training he had put into preparing for that day because, in the end, he lost his reward. He forfeited the gold medal and lost credit for breaking a world record. None of us want to start out strong when going after our call for God and end up disqualified.

7 DIMENSIONS TO FULFILLING YOUR CALL

How to Avoid the Pitfalls

God does not want us to fall short in any area of our lives. Establishing who we are on the wrong foundation will dilute our focus and cloud our pursuit. We can evade these pitfalls by our wholehearted pursuit of understanding our position in Christ. In this dimension, we will discover how God defines who we are. This definition is the springboard for everything we do for the kingdom. It determines what drives us. It influences our motivation, clarifies our objectives, and positions us to succeed.

Jesus recognized the importance of having a proper definition. For that reason, He addressed it head on with the disciples before they were fully released into their own ministries. He wanted to make sure they pursued the right thing.

In Matthew 16:13–19, Jesus brought attention to this matter by asking the disciples a series of questions that set the stage for unveiling to them their true identity. He used Peter as the example. Through this dialogue between Jesus and the disciples, I believe God wants us to see upon what the core of who we are is founded. Let's walk through this exciting moment in the life of Peter and the disciples.

> When Jesus came into the region of Caesarea Philippi, He asked His disciples, saying, "Who do men say that I, the Son of Man, am?" So they said, "Some say John the Baptist, some Elijah, and others Jeremiah or one of the prophets." He said to them, "But who do you say that I am?" Simon Peter answered and said, "You are the Christ, the Son of the living God." Jesus answered and said to him, "Blessed are you, Simon Bar-Jonah, for flesh and blood has not revealed this to you, but My Father who is in heaven. And I also say to you that you are Peter, and on this rock I will build My church, and the gates

of Hades shall not prevail against it. And I will give you the keys of the kingdom of heaven, and whatever you bind on earth will be bound in heaven, and whatever you loose on earth will be loosed in heaven."
—Matthew 16:13–19 NKJV

Jesus wanted the disciples to have an accurate picture of who they were. To do that, first He had to evaluate how they perceived Him. Why? Because He knew that how they defined Him would be a direct indicator of how they defined themselves. So He asked a question, "Who do men say that I, the Son of Man, am?" Peter's response was, "Some say," but then Jesus turned around and asked, "Who do *you* say that I am?" In essence, Jesus was saying, "I know what others are saying, but what are you saying within your own heart?" His goal was to break through any limited perceptions.

Misguided Perceptions

In Matthew 16:13–14, Jesus addressed, what I consider, three misguided perceptions. A misguided perception is when our personal assessments conflict with a Heavenly revelation. It is important to differentiate between these perceptions because Proverbs 23:7 says that your perception of yourself will guide you like a compass. Note the following perceptions:

1. **Identifying ourselves based on others' viewpoints.** This first misconception was reflected in the disciples' initial response of "some say." This perspective revealed to Jesus that the disciples would potentially define themselves based on what others said or thought. Our potential will be suffocated and our self-confidence will be undermined when our perception of who we are is rooted in what others say

about us. We don't have to ever accept any negative, pre-defined attitudes from others. Too often, we look for the approval of others before we are willing to go after what God is saying to us. Remember, people may label us based on their own assessment, but God defines us based on His purpose for us.

2. **Identifying ourselves based on our gifts and talents.** This perception was revealed by Peter's response, "Some say John the Baptist." John the Baptist was an incredible preacher, and like John, Jesus also had an extraordinary preaching and teaching gift. Jesus was anointed to preach the gospel (Luke 4:18). He preached with such authority and power, he attracted massive crowds, hence, the disciples were attempting to define Jesus by His gifts.

    When our perception of who we are is rooted in our gifts, we can be detoured from the true path until we find ourselves stranded emotionally and spiritually. In his book *Attitude Is Everything*, Keith Harrell tells his story of having a successful basketball career from childhood through college. Because of his incredible basketball talent, his primary pursuit was to play in the NBA. However, on the day of the draft, the phone call he expected never came. He continued to express that his whole life revolved around that dream, and when it didn't happen, he stated, "My self-confidence and self-esteem took a dive."[4] In his book *Leadership from the Inside Out*, Kevin Cashman comments, "When one's purpose and identity is based on external results, then life becomes fragile and at risk."[5] You are more than what your gifts and talents reveal.

3. **Identifying ourselves based on our function or role.** Peter's final response was, "Some [say] Elijah,

and others Jeremiah or one of the prophets." They recognized Jesus as a prophet, and therefore, the disciples were attempting to define Jesus based on a function. The prophetic mantle was another manifestation of the anointing on Jesus' life. Even those outside the covenant of God like the Samaritan woman, perceived Jesus as a prophet.

Unfortunately, to define ourselves based on roles we play, can lead to an identity crisis. In their book *Cornerstones for Calling*, Graves, Addington, and Womack emphasize that "individuals also may encounter problems separating themselves from their roles ... They may not understand that what they do is not the same as who they are."[6] Remember, the role does not define you as an individual, but rather, your individuality defines the role.

Jesus' assessment of the disciples was correct—they had the wrong perception. Of course, He already knew that, but he wanted them to see it for themselves. He wanted to enlarge their thinking. The impact we make for the kingdom of God will be a direct reflection of how we define ourselves. The core of who Jesus was, was not based on what others thought, his gifts, or position, but rather, on how God defined Him. As we continue the passage in Matthew 16, we see that Jesus transformed the disciples' definition of themselves by unveiling three spiritual revelations.

Revelation Impacts Perceptions

A revelation is like a new idea, and new ideas take us to new horizons. For example, there have been three technological ideas that have revolutionized America's society. The first was the advent of the computer. This marked the beginning of the Information Age, closing the chapter to the Industrial Revolution. The first computer, invented in the 1940's, was so immense, with so many components and wires, that it weighed over 700 pounds and filled an entire building. Then, later, in the early 1980's, the personal computer (PC) was invented. Now, PCs are much smaller and faster than those original monoliths. Despite the fact that the first computer filled a room, PCs are now small enough to fit into a backpack or purse, like a laptop or tablet, and they continue to get smaller.

The second technological idea that came along was called computer software. All kinds of software became available that allowed one to create letters, do taxes, write a will, keep finances, compose one's own music and videos, etc. Software made the computer usable.

Finally, the third technological idea that was invented was called the Internet. The Internet, which is a network of millions of computers linked together, created the information highway. The Internet connected the world together. We now have instant access to all kinds of information. What was once exclusive to our public libraries, private or public companies, or even governments around the world, is now available at the click of a button from our home PC by way of the Internet. We can bank online so we don't have to wait in long lines, and we can work from home and still be global because we can collaborate with others around the world. We can shop online and have products delivered to our front door. It is estimated that there were over 2.6 billion Internet users at the end of 2011, which represented 32.7% of the world's population.[7] In today's culture, having access to the Internet means expediency.

These three technologies, the computer, computer software, and the Internet, now accepted as modern day conveniences, have changed the face of the world as we know it. Steven Covey calls a phenomenon of this type a paradigm shift. This is something that occurs when a new idea is embraced and totally changes one's way of thinking.

Jesus' message to Peter and the disciples was a paradigm shift. If Peter could embrace an altogether new concept of who he was, he could step into a new day for his life.

The three revelations that Jesus unveiled to unleash the disciples in their calling, represent a three-fold chord. How these revelations compliment each other is similar to what Ecclesiastes 4:12 describes as a three-fold chord that cannot be easily broken. The dynamic that takes place when three chords are intertwined to form a rope, produces a strength beyond what each can do independent of the other. The disciples' comprehension of these three revelations would make them unstoppable in their calling.

To expand on Jesus' conversation with the disciples in Matthew 16, let's pause for moment and skip to John chapter 1, when Jesus met Peter for the first time. It was here that Jesus unveiled the first of these three revelations.

A New Name

> He first findeth his own brother Simon, and saith unto him, we have found the Messias, which is, being interpreted, the Christ. And he brought him to Jesus. And when Jesus beheld him, he said, Thou art Simon the son of Jona: thou shalt be called Cephas, which is by interpretation, A stone.
> —John 1:41–42 KJV

The first revelation is revealed—*the revelation of the stone*. John chapter 1 shows how Peter's original name was Simon. At this point, let's refer to him as Simon until that name is changed.

Notice the order. John introduced Simon to Jesus. When Jesus saw him for the first time, He immediately discerned where Simon was spiritually. Simon was a man with great potential for the kingdom but had a narrow perception. We know this because Jesus first acknowledged him as "Simon, son of Jona."

Jesus uncovered the significance of his name in two areas—the natural and the spiritual. First, Simon, named by his parents as they knew him, represented what's earthly. It signified a natural man with no spiritual revelation. And because he lacked revelation, he had yet to tap into his true purpose. This teaches us that a person without Godly insight of who he really is, is limited in terms of what he can do for the kingdom of God. Without exposure to the will, plan, and purposes of God, the maximum that person can achieve for the kingdom's sake will be a product of his own carnal desires.

Then Jesus gave Simon a new name. In essence, Jesus was saying, "Simon, I'm going to put you in touch with who you really are. I'm going to tell you what Heaven knows about you." Then Jesus proclaimed, "Thou art Cephas" or Peter, meaning "stone!" This new name had spiritual significance.

In 2009, a Jamaican track and field runner named Usain Bolt held both the world and Olympic record as the fastest man in the 100-, 200-, and 400-meter relay races. The media called him "Lightning Bolt" because he was considered the fastest man in the world, a nickname based on his accomplishments.[8]

Today we call it a nickname, but when Jesus added Peter to Simon, the Bible refers to that new name as a surname. A surname is more significant because it is patterned after one's character or authority. When Jesus called him "Peter," Jesus was revealing how his name had been authorized in heaven, and was now a reflection of what God knew about him. In Acts 10:5, an angel appeared to a man named Cornelius, in a vision, and told to him, "Now send men to Joppa, and call for one Simon, whose surname is Peter." Here we see that all of heaven recognized Simon by his new name—Peter. This confirms that his name was not a typical nickname, but rather, it had spiritual significance. What heaven knew about Simon was totally different from his spontaneous and impatient nature. Heaven recognized him as Peter, a consistent and rock-like character. Jesus was "calling those things that be not as though they were."

Finally, and most importantly, Jesus calling him "Peter" indicated there was something about being called "stone" that was pointing him to the core of who he really was. The stone was an analogy, and in that moment, Simon had been redefined. It was as if Jesus had christened him into the kingdom. Simon perceived himself as an ordinary fisherman, but Jesus was preparing him to be a fisher of men. The impact Simon could make on the earth was contingent upon the level of revelation that he walked in concerning a stone. Unfortunately, his first encounter with Jesus wasn't enough for him to walk in the fullness of that revelation. Jesus knew He had to re-frame the disciple's perception, but at this point, it had not been revealed to them who Christ was beyond being the Messiah.

More Revelation Unfolds

It's estimated that by 2015, there will be over two billion personal computers in use.[9] Again, the number of computers sold today is not just because they are smaller, lighter, cheaper, and faster, but rather, because software has unlocked the potential of the computer. PC hardware alone is inconsequential. In the same way, Jesus knew that Simon needed the second revelation to release the potential of the first—the stone.

Now turn back with me to Matthew 16:13–19, where Jesus is standing before the disciples to finish what He started in John chapter 1. In response to Jesus' question of, "Who do you say that I am?" Simon finally responded, "You are the Christ, the Son of the living God." Something different happened. At that moment, the second revelation was revealed—*the revelation of Christ.*

God opened Simon's spiritual eyes to recognize Jesus not only as the Messiah but also as the Son of the Living God. He went beyond defining Jesus by what others were saying, by His gift, or His function but was able to comprehend who Jesus really was.

Peter, the Blessed Man

> Jesus answered and said to him, "Blessed are you, Simon Bar-Jonah, for flesh and blood has not revealed this to you, but My Father who is in heaven. And I also say to you that you are Peter."
> —Matthew 16:17–18 NKJV

This was a critical moment for the disciples and an exciting moment for Jesus because of this second revelation. Out of this excitement, Jesus called Simon "blessed." Blessed means empowered to prosper. This natural man just received a revelation from God, and now he's empowered to walk in the revelation of Peter—the stone.

The Stone Revealed

From this point forward, we will refer to Simon as Peter. In John chapter 1, Christ was revealed as the Lamb of God, but in Matthew 16, the revelation of who Jesus was, was taken a step further, as He was revealed as the Son of the Living God. In other words, Peter could not see himself as stone (1st revelation) until he saw Christ as Son (2nd revelation).

Now, let's go further. Why did the revelation of Christ make the difference? We see the relevance of this question in the meaning of Peter's name.

To illustrate, I want to use the earth as an example and the process it goes through to produce a unique type of rock. The earth is made up of three layers. The first layer is the inner core, which is the center of the earth. The second layer is the outer layer called the crust or the earth's surface. The third layer lies beneath the earth's surface and is called the mantle, which makes up about two-thirds of the earth's mass.[10]

Because of high temperatures and seismic activity that take place deep within the mantle, fragment pieces of mantle crystallize into what's known as carbons. Through volcanic eruptions called magmas, these carbon elements are lifted to the earth's surface at a rapid pace. When these volcanic eruptions occur, it's as if the earth is literally burping, and when it burps, these carbons are elevated near the surface of the earth only to be discovered. Why this is so interesting is that these carbons produce a substance known as diamonds.[11]

I call this the Rock Principle. Jesus introduced this principle to the disciples to reveal the relevance of Peter's name.

> And I also say to you that you are Peter, and on this rock I will build My church.
> —Matthew 16:18 NKJV

Jesus called Simon "Peter." The Greek word for Peter is "Petros," which means "fragment piece of rock or stone," not fragment as in inferior but as a part of the whole, an extension of or a representation of the source. The Greek word for rock is "petra," which means "mass of rock or foundation." Here Jesus is figuratively speaking of Himself. So Peter, the fragment piece of rock or stone, is literally an extension, a reflection, and a representation of the mass of Rock—Christ. Christ is the foundation for the stone. The analogy is made clear. Just like a fragment piece of a diamond's identity is tied to the mantle of the earth, Peter's identity (the fragment piece of rock or stone) was tied to Christ—the mass of rock.

Secondly, our identity is tied to Christ. The fragment rock described here is also figurative for the Church. Let's further explore the text: "Upon this rock I will build My church." The Greek word for Church is "ekklesia," which means "the calling out of an assembly."

Now "ekklesia" is made up of two words, *ek* meaning "the point whence action or motion proceeds," which denotes origin or source. The second half of the word comes from the word, *kaleo*, which means "to call or command." God called the Church forth out of something and that something was Christ, the foundation. The Church was birthed out of the redemptive work of Christ. God summoned the Church from the mass of Rock.

So like Peter, the Church is a fragment rock or stone. We're called to be an extension of Christ, the Mass of Rock. This analogy of the rock reveals this principle: Our identification of who we are is rooted in Christ. Colossians 3:3 tell us, "Your life is hid with Christ in God." Since our identity is tied to Him, then like Peter and the disciples, we must understand who He is.

The Father's Definition

To understand who Christ is, begins with understanding how God defined Him. God defined Him as His Son in Matthew 3:17, "And lo a voice from heaven, saying, This is my beloved Son, in whom I am well pleased." This tells us that the source of Jesus' individuality was not rooted in His role as a prophet, preacher, or teacher. We know He had great gifts and talents. He was a healer and miracle worker, but His security in Himself was not contingent on the things He did. The source of His fulfillment was not dependent on His trade as a carpenter or in His ability to draw a crowd. His identity was rooted in His relationship with the Father as His Son.

God opened Peter's eyes to see how He defined Jesus as the Son of the Living God. This is where we experience what God has to say about who we are, because Peter being called a stone was an analogy of what it means to be a son. Sonship is our identity. God Himself defined us, and our definition is holy and untouched by man. This principle will diffuse any misguided perceptions, enable us to avoid pitfalls, and help set the focus for every believer to go after what matters to God the most—our relationship with Him. With this understanding, now we can move forward to the third revelation.

The Third Revelation

Finally, just as the third technological idea, the Internet, unleashed the power of PCs and software, likewise, because of the first two revelations, this third revelation unleashed the power of the disciples, which is the *revelation of purpose*.

Built to Prevail

> I will build My church, and the gates of Hades shall not prevail against it. And I will give you the keys of the

kingdom of heaven, and whatever you bind on earth will be bound in heaven, and whatever you loose on earth will be loosed in heaven.
—Matthew 16:18–19 NKJV

Out of the mass of rock, Jesus called forth His Church and revealed its purpose—to take its position of authority and rule the earth. We must live, move, have our existence in Christ. Upon the revelation that Christ is the foundation, the Church is being established. God is not building a physical structure but a people becoming who God made them to be, a people who understand their purpose. By giving the Church the keys of the kingdom, God empowered us to accomplish the heavenly vision.

Jesus also emphasized that there will be opposition. His statement, "the gates of hell shall not prevail," infers friction. Friction is a result of motion or movement. It's amazing how the Church shines through opposition. We're just like that fragment piece of mantle, being conditioned by the intense temperatures in the depths of the earth. We are undergoing the pressurization process that causes the diamond in us to emerge. Romans 8:18–19 tells us, "For I consider that the sufferings of this present time are not worthy to be compared with the glory which shall be revealed in us. For the earnest expectation of the creation eagerly waits for the revealing of the sons of God."[12]

Satan is afraid of you walking in revelation of your calling as a son, because when you do, he knows you will advance the kingdom of God in the earth in demonstration and power. We're called to take back from the kingdom of darkness what rightfully belongs to God. The earth belongs to God and everything in it.

Note the order of revelations: the revelation of Christ, the revelation of stone, and now, the revelation of purpose.

This is why a three-fold chord cannot break easily. With the unfolding of these revelations, the disciples fulfilled their purpose. We are still being impacted by their results.

Oliver Wendell Homes once said, "Man's mind, stretched by a new idea, never goes back to its original dimensions." When God deposits a revelation, we're never the same. Our spirit is enlarged and our lives are changed forever. Our minds are now influenced to recognize that we can do all things through Christ for God's glory.

God wants to unlock the revelation of who you are as a son. As you understand what this means, then you are on your way to walking in revelation of your purpose that can impact every arena of your life. Only then can you confidently fulfill God's call. Now let's further explore the importance of our identity as sons of God.

Chapter 3

7 Principles

1. Making our service to God our number one priority doesn't mean we've made God our number one priority.

2. When we're mission-minded only, we set ourselves up to fail at reaching all that God has in store for us.

3. In this dimension of our call—understanding our position in Christ—we will discover how God defines who we are, which is the springboard for everything we do for the kingdom.

4. The role does not define you as an individual, but rather, your individuality defines the role.

5. Without exposure to the will, plan, and purposes of God, the maximum that person can achieve for the kingdom's sake will be a product of his own carnal desires.

6. Our identification of who we are is rooted in Christ since our identity is tied to Him, then like Peter and the disciples, we must grasp who He is.

7. We're just like that fragment piece of mantle, being conditioned by the intense temperatures in the depths of the earth; we are undergoing the pressurization process that causes the diamond in us to emerge.

CHAPTER 4

THE CALL SETS THE PRIORITY

But as many as received him, to them gave he power to become the sons of God, even to them that believe on his name.
—John 1:12 KJV

Behold, what manner of love the Father hath bestowed upon us, that we should be called the sons of God.
—1 John 3:1 KJV

To fulfill the call on our lives from the right perspective, we have to give priority to who we are. This personal testimony by Retired U.S. Army Major Darrell G. Harris, illustrates this key point.

> I was a lieutenant platoon leader, and it used to drive my leaders crazy when I'd go out for lunch and read my Bible. They would find me in my car or under some tree, catching shade and reading God's Word. They would ask, "Lieutenant, what are you doing?"

"I'm reading my Bible. I'm studying."

"Well you haven't completed your CAB leader's course yet, so how come you're not studying that? How come you're not studying how to apply tourniquets and give IVs to your fellow soldiers when they get dehydrated?"
"Well, I do study that. While I'm not setting aside *this* time to study that, I am ready to do that."

"You're just different. You're not the typical Lieutenant," they responded.

"You have to remember, sir, I'm a soldier. That's what I do. I am going to prepare people for battle because lives depend on it. I'm going to do it very well. I'll be one of the best lieutenants you ever had. That is what I do but not who I am. I'm God's man. I'm His servant. While I'm out doing these lieutenant things, people come to me with real needs that you are not aware of, and it's God who helps me serve them in what they really need." Because I honored God in this way and in the 3rd Armory Cavalry Regiment, I had the second most combat ready platoon. Because I gave priority to who I am, God made sure that what I did succeeded.
—Darrell G. Harris, Major, US Army (Ret.)

God's description of Jesus wasn't that He was a great preacher, or that He did great things. God declared Jesus as His Son "in whom [He] [was] well pleased" (Matthew 3:13). How was Jesus so successful in pleasing God and fulfilling His call? The secret to His success was that He built His ministry on a proper foundation. He gave priority to who He was, which was established upon His relationship with the Father. He did ministry out of relationship with God, as His Son.

In Jesus' case, the ministry and the man could not be separated. Ministry was an outflow of who He was as the Son of God. In other words, He didn't do ministry during the day, i.e. healing the sick, preaching the Gospel, touching people's lives, and then at night, as if it were a garment, pull off His Sonship and behave in a way that was inconsistent to being God's Son. His love for God reflected on and off the center stage. He had character and integrity. The same anointing on His life was in His life. He was the Son of God, modeling the way for us to live as sons.

So how should we define ourselves? As missionaries only? As prophets only? No matter what occupation or calling we may have, we have a greater definition in God's eyes.

When you accepted Jesus Christ as Chief Shepherd, you were authorized to walk as a son of God (John 1:12). Galatians 3:26 says we are all "sons of God through faith in Christ Jesus." In Greek, "son" means "child of God." So whether you are male or female, you are included in the term, "sons of God." You are a new creation in Christ because God has given you the authority to become His child. You have unrestricted rights, privileges, and responsibilities as a child of God.

We are not just called to do the works of Jesus, but our lives are to be an extension of who we are as sons of the Living God. This Second Dimension of the Call—Understanding our Position in Christ, is one of most important elements of your call because this dimension will help you understand that you are a son before you are a preacher or missionary. Remember, before you could step into your calling, you had to become a child of God first. The new birth was the process by which the Spirit of God transformed you from darkness to light. So, being a son is primary; being a preacher is secondary, because your role in the body of Christ is temporal, but being a son is eternal.

On what foundation is your ministry built? In Luke 6:48, the house that was built on the rock, stood the test of time. When as a son, you build ministry out of relationship with God, then you are building God's kingdom on the right foundation. Your foundation will affect what you pursue and everything you do. God never intends that you separate ministry from the person. He intends for ministry to be an outflow of your relationship with the Lord. According to Pastor Allan Meyer, "By creation our world was designed to revolve around relationship with the Father. This relationship was intended to be the center of our existence, keeping everything in perspective."[1]

The preacher in you is God's gift to the world, but this world will some day pass away. On the other hand, being a son in the kingdom of God will never end. You may be a minister in public, but you are still a son of God in private when no one is looking. You cannot substitute the thrill of accomplishing things in exchange for the continual experience of God's presence and allow that experience to impact your behavior. Your mission from God is critical, but your relationship with God is irreplaceable.

Ephesians 1:16–17, shows us how Paul prayed this over the saints of Ephesus. "I pray for you constantly, asking God, the glorious Father of our Lord Jesus Christ, to give you wisdom to see clearly and really understand who Christ is and all that he has done for you."[2] Walking in the fullness of who you are as a son is contingent upon you knowing who Jesus is as Son.

God never intended that we stay at the same spiritual level from one year to the next. Instead, He intends for us to experience an ongoing transformation. The disciples were transformed each time Jesus taught them, and teaching them was a daily occurrence. Keeping our primary focus on our relationship with God will enable us to keep a persistent focus on our position in Christ, so that we continuously conform to His Image.

Why Is It Significant to Conform?

> And we know that all things work together for good to those who love God, to those who are the called according to His purpose. For whom He foreknew, He also predestined to be conformed to the image of His Son, that He might be the firstborn among many brethren. Moreover whom He predestined, these He also called; whom He called, these He also justified; and whom He justified, these He also glorified.
> —Romans 8:28–30 NKJV

As sons, we're called to conform to the image of Christ. The Greek word conform is "summorphos," which means "to have the same form as another, to be fashioned like unto."[3] Nature experiences a similar process called metamorphosis. For example, we appreciate the beauty of the butterfly. What's interesting is that the butterfly wasn't born with wings. Nature transforms the caterpillar, an earthbound, crawling insect, into a graceful, winged, flying creature.

Once we're in Christ, we experience a similar type of change. According to Second Corinthians 5:17, "This means that anyone who belongs to Christ has become a new person. The old life is gone; a new life has begun!"[4] This verse literally means our nature is transformed to become like Christ.

Another example of nature that reveals this phenomenon is the life of a frog. When a frog is born, it is a tiny tadpole, living, swimming, and breathing water through gills. But when it reaches adulthood, it becomes a land creature breathing air through its lungs. There's an abrupt change in the body, cells, behavior, and habitat of this mammal.

So from a kingdom perspective, to conform implies this type of change because our end results will look nothing like the beginning. The butterfly looks nothing like the caterpillar. The frog looks nothing like the tadpole. Our new nature looks nothing like our old nature but like unto Christ. God determined that we would do great exploits and be fashioned like unto Him, while doing these great exploits. It is the wonderful process of conforming.

We conform to the image of Christ in three ways. First, when we repent of sin and accept Jesus Christ as our personal Lord and Savior, immediately we are transformed spiritually. Our spirit is made alive unto God and we are made the righteousness of God in Christ Jesus.

The second part of us, our soul, is being changed. The soul consists of our mind, will, intellect, and emotions—our character. We are transformed by renewing our minds, which affects each aspect of our soul (Romans 12:1–2). This part of us is not immediately transformed. This transformation is an ongoing process that will continue until Jesus returns.

In the amplified version of Romans 8:29, Paul teaches that we are to be "molded into His image and share inwardly his likeness. Christ represents what renewed humanity is supposed to look and act like."[5] The Holy Spirit, working the Word in us, fashions us into the image of Christ by molding our character, motives, thoughts, and feelings after Christ's likeness (Ephesians 4:24; Colossians 3:10).

The third part of us, our physical bodies, gives way to the last and final process of conformation. The kind of body Jesus has now in heaven is His glorified body. When He returns, our bodies will undergo a transformation process in which our physical state will be like His. Our sin nature will be completely removed forever, and our bodies, which are subject to death, will become incorruptible; death will lose its power (1 Corinthians 15:51–54). Conforming to the image of Jesus Christ is a by-product of our relationship with Him. This means we have to connect to God as our source. Our connection to the Source is seen in John 15:1, 4–5, which says, "I am the true vine, and my Father is the husbandman ... As the branch cannot bear fruit of itself, except it abide in the vine; no more can ye, except ye abide in me ... for without me ye can do nothing" (KJV).

There was an instance, while I was writing this book using my laptop, when the battery died, and then, of course, it immediately powered off. What was so interesting is that my power adapter was plugged into the surge protector, and that was plugged into the wall outlet, so it didn't make sense there was no power. After investigating, I discovered that I was plugged into a bad socket on the surge protector. When I plugged the cord into a different outlet, the right source, immediately, electrical power began to flow, my laptop powered back on, and the battery continued to charge. Although this is a simple analogy, it reminds us that because of our humanity, we have to plug into the right source. If not, we'll find ourselves drained of life and spiritual energy.

In John 15, Jesus expresses that He is the vine and that we are the branches tied into Him. We have to stay in living communion with Him because the branch (which represents every believer) is unable to bear fruit by itself. Like the laptop, we have to stay plugged in. In other words, we have to stay connected to Jesus as our life source to keep experiencing God's transformational power in our lives. As we do, elements of our lives are literally adjusted, tweaked, and modified to fit and take on His nature and His instinctive way of living and acting.

The Well of Life

Jesus described Himself as a well; the water of life in John 4, the source we continue returning to, to quench all the parched areas of our lives. If we don't, we also can become what Jeremiah described in Jeremiah 2:13 as broken cisterns.

There is a difference between a cistern and a well. A cistern was a man-made hole in the ground or rock designed to capture rainwater, in which case, the storing of water was dependent on an external source—rain. A well is something that has an internal water source underground. When we turn away from God to other things for fulfillment and satisfaction, we become like broken cisterns that can't hold water. We have no internal source. We cannot hold or contain the peace, joy, purpose, and fulfillment we were summoned to have by letting God spring up from the inside. Jesus Christ is the source of all we need. Our lives are hid in Christ. It is in Christ that we live, move, and have our being. We must stay connected to the source.

Cover Up

A friend of mine told me story about his project to remodel his kitchen. His home was over sixty years old and had been in his family a long time. Based on a limited budget, he planned to apply a new coat of paint and replace the cabinetry, appliances, and flooring. He was willing to overlook the fact that his kitchen had uneven floors.

He hired a contractor to help him start what he thought would be a simple project. As they began to remove the old tiles, the uneven parts of the floor really became apparent. Reluctantly, they kept peeling the old tiles away until the contractor finally noticed something.

"You might want to see this, Mr. J."

THE CALL SETS THE PRIORITY

"Oh no, not something else! That's the third issue you've pointed out today! Remember, all I want is a simple job: only paint, cabinets, appliances, and some tile, that's it! That's the goal!"

"Mr. J, if you really want to do this right, you've got to face the facts. It may hurt now, but in the end, it will be worth it. Pay now or pay later. Either way, you're gonna pay."

Mr. J relented. "Understood. Go ahead and show me the problem."

"Well, sir, look where I'm shining the light. Ya see it? Look at these damaged floor joists. Now look over here. See the corrosion in these concrete pillars? It's not the floor that's your problem; it's the foundation."

My friend took a deep sigh and paused. "What do I need to do?" he asked.

"It's beyond my expertise, Mr. J. You're gonna need a foundation expert. I can recommend someone if you don't know one."

My friend was disheartened by the news. What started out to be a simple kitchen remodeling effort ended up being a major reconstruction project.

For as long as my friend had been in the home, the kitchen floor had always been uneven. Unfortunately, this uneven surface was merely a symptom of a deeper problem. In the same way, sooner or later, our issues will be revealed. We can't hide from God, what lies beneath the surface of our hearts.

In Genesis, after Adam and Eve sinned, the glory of God was cut off, and sin left them uncovered. As a consequence, they experienced fear, insecurity, inadequacy, shame, and guilt. They hid themselves from God and tried to cover their shame with fig leaves, hoping that God couldn't see how vulnerable their sin had left them. We can't hide anything from God either. Keeping secrets from God will only hinder our union with Him and impede the transformation process.

> But we all, with open face beholding as in a glass the glory of the Lord, are changed into the same image from glory to glory, even as by the Spirit of the Lord.
> —2 Corinthians 3:18 NKJV

By beholding Christ with an open face, we unveil ourselves much like when a woman removes her makeup, exposing her countenance, and we become vulnerable again. We can portray ourselves one way to others, but God sees us for who we really are. Anger, unforgiveness, insecurities, fear, disobedience, and the like are all symptoms of what needs further unveiling and transformation. The more we suppress and push away our issues, the more it will cost us in the long run.

Colossians 3:10 continues, "You are living a brand new kind of life that is continually learning more and more of what is right, and trying constantly to be more and more like Christ who created this new life within you."[6] Spending time with God and maintaining a repentant heart continues this transformation and takes us from glory to glory. This is the glory that Adam lost but that is now being restored in us. To move from glory to glory requires our focus.

Like Holding a Mirror

"Honey!" my wife shouted. "Come quickly."

I ran from our bedroom into the hallway. Then my wife motioned to me to approach quietly.

"What is she looking at?" she muttered in a loud whisper. Then she directed my attention to another room. It was my 5-year-old daughter, lying across the bottom bunk

THE CALL SETS THE PRIORITY

bed in our son's room. We weren't sure why she was staring into the air, but she was lying on her stomach enjoying herself. Her knees were bent and her feet were swinging in the air, moving about as if her toes were playing a little game. Her chin rested in the palm of her hands while her elbows were propped on the bed. She laughed and giggled staring at what appeared to be an empty corner of the room. This particular corner had no pictures, no toys, no child's artwork—the kids hadn't christened that side of the wall with any crayon artwork yet. She was carrying on as if something or someone was there and had her full attention.

My wife and I looked at each other in amazement. My wife stepped one foot into the room, turning to my daughter.

"What are you looking at?" my wife asked.

"The angel," my daughter responded.

"What angel?" my wife asked again.

"Mom, can't you see the angel?" Our mouths dropped in amazement. Unfortunately, we didn't see any angel. In fact, we saw nothing but apparently my daughter did. Whether it was an angel or her imagination, it captivated her attention.

God wants to captivate our attention. To "behold as in a glass" figuratively means looking in a mirror to see a reflection. It means to gaze and to look at something with attentiveness.

Looking into this mirror represents us giving God our full attention in times of prayer, worship, reading, and meditating on His Word. While in His presence, He reveals Himself, and that's when we begin to see the reflection. Initially, we're not seeing our image in this mirror but Christ's. The irony is that we can't see Him if we don't unveil ourselves. And yet the more we stare at Him, through His reflection, He reproduces Himself in us. It is then that we start to see ourselves as we should be. The goal is not about self-revelation but rather revelation of Jesus. The outcome is that we "are changed into the same image from glory to glory, even as by the Spirit of the Lord."

Selwyn Hughes describes this concept as the law of photography. He said, "The angle of incidence equals the angle of reflection. If you want a full-face reproduction, you must look full into the camera."[7] As we look full into Christ, the Holy Spirit will gradually transform us into the image we set our gaze upon. Physically we are not changing, but inwardly our character, behavior, and thoughts will be transformed and will impact our actions.

Now God's glory can shine through us. Jesus touched the lives of those He encountered, so those who encounter God's people should experience a difference. The world should experience God's glory by their experience with our character. Encountering Christ as Savior is only the beginning. Pursuing Christ as Son positions us to fulfill this Second Dimension of the Call—Understanding Our Position in Christ.

Chapter 4

7 Principles

1. You are a new creation in Christ because God has given you the authority to become His child. You have unrestricted rights, privileges, and responsibilities as a child of God.

2. Your mission from God is critical, but your relationship with God is irreplaceable.

3. With our primary focus on our relationship with God, we will keep a persistent focus on our position in Christ, so that we continuously conform to His Image.

4. We have to stay connected to Jesus as our life source to keep experiencing God's transformational power in our lives.

5. Keeping secrets from God will only hinder our union with Him and impede the transformation process.

6. The irony is that we can't see God if we don't unveil ourselves. The more we stare at Him, through this reflection, the more He reproduces Himself in us. It is then, we start to see ourselves as we should be.

7. As we look full into Christ, the Holy Spirit will gradually transform us into the image we set our gaze upon. Physically, we are not changing, but inwardly, our character, behavior, and thoughts will be transformed and will impact our actions.

THE THIRD DIMENSION: THE RIGHT PURSUIT

CHAPTER 5

WHAT DID JESUS PURSUE?

For I came down from heaven, not to do mine own will, but the will of him that sent me.
—John 6:38 KJV

"GOT A MINUTE?" he asked.

"Yes sir," I responded.

"Can you meet me in my office in about five minutes?" he continued.

"Sure, let me finish up with this customer, unload this last box, and I'll be right there." I quickly pushed the handcart behind the Sporting Good's counter and headed toward the opposite end of the store.

The office of Mr. C, our store manager, was the last door down the long hallway, in the back of the store. As I started my journey toward that office, I wondered why Mr. C needed to talk to me. Did I do something wrong? If I did, it didn't make sense. I just recently got my performance review, one of the best ones yet. My manager's comments proved

I was a team player, great with customers, and finished my projects on time. So what was this meeting all about?

I had been working this job ever since high school and had received seven years of great performance evaluations. I committed myself to every sacrifice to make my department successful. I was responsible for the toys and sporting goods departments. Also, I was attending junior college part-time but work was my priority. I occasionally missed a class or two when volunteers at work were needed. I'd raised my hands at any opportunity to make more money by working extra hours. Even if it was odd hours or odd assignments, I was up for the challenge. When sales were down and our store didn't have enough hours to distribute to part-timers, as a full-time associate, I gave up some of my hours just so I could be a blessing. I understood the financial struggles some of my co-workers were experiencing.

My boss greeted me as I entered his office. "Please sit down."

"Yes sir."

"You are a great asset to this company."

"Thank you."

Then he handed me a folded piece of paper he pulled from an interoffice envelope. "Please take a look at the note from corporate. What you see is the total number of hours worked in the previous year and a half. It averages less than forty hours per week."

"Yes sir, I guess it makes sense. Many times, I gave up hours so others could work."

"Yes, I know. And that was very admirable of you, but unfortunately," then he took a long pause, "the system just calculates the annual hours, so when it's less than 2080 work hours for the year, automatically, the system drops you from full-time to part-time status."

"Ok, what does that mean?"

"It means you've lost all your benefits. No more medical, no more retirement, no more 401(k), and no more vacation time."

"What?" I really didn't understand the retirement part but no medical or paid time off and no free 401(k) money?

"Sorry, you've been dropped to part-time status with no benefits, and there is nothing I can do." Back to work, I thought as I left Mr. C's office.

My handcart squealed and juddered as I pressed my way back to the stockroom for more merchandise to restock the shelves. But the noise from that handcart couldn't drown out the conversation Mr. C and I just had. His voice kept reverberating in my head, "No benefits…nothing I can do." What's next for me? I contemplated as I slowly loaded another box onto the handcart. I had a decision to make.

That day was a turning point for me. It was then that I realized the importance of a college degree. I knew college wasn't for everybody, but for me, I felt that if I didn't make school a priority, my financial future would be a struggle. This little talk with my boss motivated me to stop procrastinating. It was at that moment that I made the decision to stop pursuing money and independence and pursue a four-year bachelor's degree. I learned later that my degree did open the doors for me to experience more opportunities than I would have experienced without the degree. School became my primary pursuit.

To pursue means to follow after in order to overtake. I pursued my bachelor's degree until I obtained it. Jesus' life exemplified what it means to pursue the kingdom of God. The right pursuit is the third dimension of the call and can be accomplished by following Jesus' pattern.

What Jesus Did Not Pursue

In order to understand what Jesus pursued, let's eliminate what He did not pursue. First, Jesus didn't pursue power and authority. He already understood the source of His authority. He said that all things were given to Him from God (John 17:7), and He constantly expressed that "the Son can do nothing of his own accord."[1] God was the source of His authority and power.

Second, Jesus did not pursue fame and prestige. Satan tried to tempt Him with the gold and glory of the world, but Jesus resisted. Popularity could not sidetrack Him. The people tried to make Him king, but Jesus knew their goal was in direct conflict with His purpose. He didn't let the crowds change His perspective of who He was as the Son of God. Jesus knew intimately the glory God had waiting for Him was greater than any title man could bestow. So when the people tried to make Him king, He avoided it and got alone with God (John 6:15). He didn't let the results of what God did through Him negatively affect His pursuit.

When receiving accolades from others, we can't forget that we are only vessels where the excellency of His power can reside. We are imperfect vessels being used by a perfect God.

Finally, Jesus didn't look to take credit for Himself but wanted all the credit to go to God. He said that the one who wants the glory for Himself is focused on Himself (John 7:18). In fact, He didn't mind sharing His power because it wasn't about Him. He delegated power and authority to his twelve disciples and later to seventy more. Then he delegated power and authority to us, the body of Christ. His life wasn't all about elevating Himself, but He was all about meeting needs and empowering the disciples to do the same.

So if Jesus wasn't pursing power, authority, fame, prestige, and all the credit, then what was His passion? What did He model for us?

Jesus' Main Priorities

> Jesus spoke these words, lifted up His eyes to heaven, and said: "Father, the hour has come. Glorify Your Son, that Your Son also may glorify You ... I have glorified You on the earth. I have finished the work which You have given Me to do."
> —John 17:1, 4 NKJV

The first pattern Jesus set was making His relationship with God His utmost priority. The very first word out of Jesus' mouth in John 17:1 was, "Father." Jesus was considered by others as a priest, prophet, and teacher, yet the perspective of the prayer in John chapter 17 was not based on any of those titles but rather, on His relationship with the Father, as His Son. Jesus was most concerned with what was on the Father's heart. The Spirit of God enabled Jesus to accomplish what the Father wanted, but His relationship as Son kept Him tuned into the Father.

As believers, our goal, on a daily basis, should be to end the day in prayer, "Father, today, I have kept Your word. I have loved as You would love. I gave of myself as You would have." Praying like this would not be the gift talking, not the evangelist in us, or the prophetic anointing, but we would be praying like Jesus, through our relationship as a son talking to our Father. Jesus' relationship with God was a priority. As a result, His works glorified the Father.

Christ Our Model

The second pattern Jesus set for us was His prayer life.

One weekend, I attended a retreat sponsored by a local ministry. The speaker shared some startling statistics; the average Christian spends three minutes a day in prayer. Whether or not these statistics had any validity, I don't know, but it was enough to get my attention. I wondered about my prayer life. I thought about how much time I spent being busy, compared to time I spent praying. Whatever it averaged out to be, I knew for me it wasn't enough.

I don't know if there is a magic number of hours we should pray in order for the things in life to fall in place for the day, but I notice when I lack spending quality time in prayer, things seem to fall apart, and I'm more frustrated. God's voice seems distant and at times, hidden. Sometimes, His will is overly difficult to discern. When we lack prayer, passion for the things of God becomes secondary, and the things of the world become more interesting.

Mark 1:35 tells us that Jesus' prayer life consisted of times when he rose "very early in the morning, while it was still dark." The verse says, "Jesus got up, left the house and went off to a solitary place, where he prayed."[2] Jesus always got alone with God. He made prayer a priority.

Prayer means to commune. Prayer for us is like gas to a car. You can't just fill your gas tank one time and expect to get everywhere you need to go. Running out of gas is no fun, especially traveling on the interstate. A consistent prayer life will keep our spiritual tanks full and keep us mobile for the kingdom.

Jesus lived in God's presence through prayer. It renewed His strength. It caused God's voice to be distinct in His ears and vibrant in His heart. Jesus received daily instructions from God through such a consistent prayer life, that He was so in sync with God, that He knew His thoughts. Prayer kept Him focused and will do so for us.

I know it's sometimes a struggle to find time to pray, but it's a battle worth fighting. The strategy is not in finding time but making time. Schedule daily time with God; maybe the first part of the day, the afternoon, or the evening. Do what works for you. The key is to spend the time. A lifestyle of communing with God will keep the passion for His presence burning in your heart.

Pursuing God's Will

> For I came down from heaven, not to do mine own will, but the will of him that sent me.
> —John 6:38 KJV

Barbecue is one of my favorite types of meals. I like to grill hot dogs, burgers, chicken, and sometimes a nice steak. There is nothing like the aroma of chicken cooking over hot flaming charcoal. Just the smell makes the wait worthwhile. The smoke flavor tingles my palette while biting into a juicy, dripping burger. It makes me think I can fill my plate with two more plus all the fixings. There's something about biting into a mesquite, hickory-smoked steak that's been grilling for hours until it's perfectly seared that brings satisfaction. (And all the brothers reading this book say "amen.")

Jesus also enjoyed meat. But the meat He referred to wasn't a steak or a burger. Jesus said, "My meat is to do the will of him that sent me, and to accomplish his work."[3] The term, "meat," was a metaphor for spiritual food. Jesus' favorite meal, that which fed Him spiritually, was God's will. Pursuing God's will was Jesus' ultimate desire and is the third pattern He set for us.

Something about doing God's will gave Jesus the ability to say, "I'm full; I'm satisfied." That energized Him. I can relate. Writing this book allowed me to experience tremendous peace, joy, and satisfaction. Every time I sat down to write, I felt God's presence because I knew writing this book was God's will for my life. We'll discuss more on this topic in chapter 12.

Loving God

Not too long ago after my family and I moved, I felt like I was doing everything I knew to do. After all, I left my job, sold our home, and relocated to Virginia because I felt God was leading me to do so. Surely, God had recognized the sacrifices I had made thus far and was about to make. It wasn't just me. I had moved my family—my wife, my two kids, and wouldn't you know it, we then learned we had a new one on the way. My God, we left a three-bedroom house and moved into my in-law's house with only a single room for my family and me. On this particular evening, I was so tired from the move and all the unpacking, I quickly fell asleep.

I dreamt that Jesus was talking to me. "Kelvin, do you love Me?"

"Yes Lord, You know I love You. I'm supposed to."

"Kelvin, do you love Me?"

"Yes Lord, I love You. Mom and Dad taught me to love You. I learned at church in Sunday school to love You."

"Kelvin, do you love Me?"

Ok, this was the third time. Why was He still asking me? "Yes," I said emphatically. "Lord, You know I love You because the Bible says to love the Lord with all your heart. It's the first commandment. I'm supposed to love You with all my strength."

Then Jesus paused and stood there, staring at me in deep silence. Then He began shaking His head from side to side as if in disappointment.

"You don't get it, do you?" He said. "I don't want you to love Me because you have to; I want you to love Me because you want to."

Then I woke up.

It was then I realized that I was expecting something from God in return for my sacrifices as if He owed me something. I know my actions were based on His leading, but what did I expect from Him as a result, recognition? Bonus points? Or did I want to please Him with my obedience? I had to come to grips with the answer to that question.

Why do you do the things you do for God? Why do you minister to other people? What is your motivation? Are you motivated by love? The fourth pattern Jesus set for us is what it means to love God.

> Have this mind in you, which was also in Christ Jesus: who, existing in the form of God, counted not the being on an equality with God a thing to be grasped, but emptied himself, taking the form of a servant, being made in the likeness of men; and being found in fashion as a man, he humbled himself, becoming obedient even unto death, yea, the death of the cross.
> —Philippians 2:5–8 ASV

First, Jesus revealed His love for God by emptying Himself. It wasn't about what He had or what He could gain. He sacrificed His life. This means we must first empty ourselves. This includes getting rid of all expectations that God is going to give us something in return for what we do for Him. I know Jesus said that whatever we give up for the sake of the gospel, God would return it (Mark 10:29, 30). We must abandon feelings of entitlement and the what's-in-it-for-me way of thinking. God doesn't owe us anything but chooses to bless us.

As parents, we pour our life into our kids. We make all the sacrifices necessary because we love them so much, we want to see them succeed in life, and we have their best interest at heart. We don't do it because we want to see them pay us back or give us something in return. Our love for our kids is unconditional, and what we do for our kids has no bounds. Jesus taught us to love God unconditionally. That dream taught me that I had to love God and obey God not because I had to, but because I wanted to.

Second, Jesus understood the Father's love because He lived in God's love. He said He loved us as God loved Him. And God loved Him before the earth was ever formed (John 17:23, 24). According to John 15:10, "When you obey me you are living in my love, just as I obey my Father and live in his love."[4] In other words, Jesus lived in God's love through His obedience. For Jesus, apart from the Father, there was no mission, purpose, or reasoning. Jesus said that if we love Him, we would do the same by keeping His commandments. Obedience is how we express our love toward God, and we live in God's love by obeying His Word.

Love in Action

Third, Jesus was the very expression of God's love, and this love motivated His actions. Compassion flowed from Him toward those who needed God. Love motivated His actions to heal the sick, feed the hungry, and reach out to those who were rejected by others. In dealing with the woman at the well, Jesus focused on her need, not on her problem. The Pharisees judged the woman caught in adultery, but Jesus refused to condemn her. Jesus didn't reject those who came to him with a need like Mary Magdalene, even while the disciples complained about her background. He loved her beyond her condition. God's love produces love for others.

I was driving on the interstate on my way home one day. As I drove under an overpass, something colorful caught my attention. It appeared to be clothes hanging right up under the overpass. Also, I saw plastic bags, boxes, and artifacts as if this underpass was a storage area. Then I saw homeless people using that part of the overpass for shelter. The weather was changing, fall temperatures were settling in, and my heart ached for them.

Over the next few days, I couldn't get that scene out of my mind. I remember thinking, *God I want to do something but I don't have the facilities to house those people. What could I do for them?*

A few days later, while walking from my office, the Lord gave me a simple idea—sleeping bags. *Oh yeah!* I thought. *If I can't house them, at least I can help them be as comfortable as possible in the setting that they're in.* So my wife and I, along with several friends, invested in sleeping bags and spent the next few days distributing them along with some food. The love of God motivated our actions.

Everything we do for God should be motivated by love, but we have to recognize that we can't produce God's love out of our own being. Selwyn Hughes commented, "Let's be done with the idea that love for God is something we work at. It issues forth in good works, of course, but it begins in contemplation of how much we are loved."[5]

Grasping God's love will fuel compassion in us and will purify our motives. When we're absorbed in His love, we're driven to see people healed, blessed, and set free. When we focus on loving God, He releases ideas, desire, and the motivation to do what we can do.

Is it possible that when we don't feel compassion for the lost or for those who are hurting, that perhaps we have fallen out of love with God? How can we successfully fulfill our calls with the absence of unconditional love? First John 3:17 asserts, "But whoever has the world's goods, and beholds his brother in need and closes his heart against him, how does the love of God abide in him?"[6] Our active love for God will produce a corresponding action toward God and toward others.

Honoring God

Jesus showed us the fifth pattern—honoring God. He did everything He was told. He taught everything God instructed Him. He honored God by finishing the work God called Him to do. He honored God as He lived a pure life in public and in private. He was tempted in all aspects but never yielded.

Likewise, we honor God when we abstain from sin. What's more exciting is the knowledge that not only does God give us the grace to abstain from sin as Jesus did, but if we do fall into sin, He also allows us to honor Him through our repentance. Proverbs 24:16 reminds us that a just man may fall, but he gets back up again. If we sin, we have Christ Jesus our advocate, waiting to restore us (1 John 1:9). God takes joy when we confess our sins; confession removes barriers in our relationship with Him.

Pleasing God

> "And He who sent Me is with Me. The Father has not left Me alone, for I always do those things that please Him."
> —John 8:29 NKJV

One day while shopping at a clothing store in a mall, I noticed quotes displayed on the wall by famous people. One quote was by a famous actor. He was asked, "What is the definition of success?" This actor replied, "I don't know the definition of success, but I do know the definition of failure—trying to please people."

Jesus didn't try to please the Pharisees and other religious people in His day. He didn't focus on Himself; He focused on pleasing God, which is the sixth pattern He set for us. If He had not pleased God, the price of our redemption would have never been paid. Likewise, if we center ourselves on others, we too, will surely displease God.

Jesus' only goal was to please the Father. The word "please" means acceptable. As you read the Gospels, you will notice that everything Jesus did was acceptable to God. God wants our actions to be acceptable.

> Let me add this, dear brothers: You already know how to please God in your daily living, for you know the commands we gave you from the Lord Jesus himself. Now we beg you—yes, we demand of you in the name of the Lord Jesus—that you live more and more closely to that ideal.
> —1 Thessalonians 4:1 TLB

In this verse in Thessalonians, Paul urges us to focus on what pleases God. Again in 1 John 3:22, we're told to, "Do the things that please him."[7] Daily we should endeavor to keep our attitude and actions acceptable to God, and ask ourselves if we are meeting our own needs or His needs by what we are doing today. Pleasing God should be our ultimate goal. It's not about perfection, but it's about going after God with our whole hearts. After all, it's His mission we're fulfilling.

Chapter 5

7 Principles

1. When receiving accolades from others, we can't forget that we are only vessels in which the excellency of His power resides. We are imperfect vessels being used by a perfect God.

2. The Spirit of God enabled Jesus to accomplish what the Father wanted, and His relationship as Son kept Him tuned into the Father.

3. Jesus received daily instructions from God through a consistent prayer life. Prayer kept Him focused and will keep us focused.

4. Obedience is how we express our love toward God, and we live in God's love by obeying His word.

5. Is it possible that when we don't feel compassion for the lost or for those hurting that we perhaps have fallen out of love with God?

6. What's more exciting is that God gives us the grace to abstain as Jesus did, and if we do fall into sin, we honor God through our repentance.

7. Daily we should endeavor to keep our attitude and actions acceptable to God and ask ourselves, "Is what I'm doing today meeting His need or my needs?"

CHAPTER 6

WHAT DID PAUL PURSUE?

That I may know Him and the power of His resurrection, and the fellowship of His sufferings, being conformed to His death.
—Philippians 3:10 NKJV

THERE IS A ministry located in Los Angeles, California, called the Dream Center, founded by Pastor Matthew Barnett. It is a non-profit, inner city ministry located in the downtown area. It's recognized as one of the leaders in outreach programs to the brokenhearted, with a focus on meeting both the physical and spiritual needs of people. Through the Dream Center, Pastor Barnett, his leadership team, and a host of volunteers, provide housing to over 750 people daily, who are in need. Their mobile food trucks feed over 40,000 people in impoverished neighborhoods on a monthly basis. Through their Adopt-A-Block program, they clean and repair homes and meet other needs of the community, reaching over 5,000 families on a weekly basis. They minister to at-risk children, single parents, and the homeless. Basically wherever there are needs, the Dream Center has over 270 ministries designed to fit and meet the need. The Dream Center is a 24-hour, 7-day-a-week, 365-day-a-year ministry.[1]

It's highly probable that the Dream Center would not be what it is today had Pastor Barnett continued to pursue what he thought was the primary focus of his calling. In his book, *The Cause Within You*, Pastor Barnett said that at the beginning of his ministry in L.A., he assumed the pastorate of Bethel Temple, a church located in an impoverished neighborhood filled with crime, drugs, and gang violence. He pursued doing what he thought a successful pastor should do. He said his life's mission was "to build God a great church."[2] But despite all his efforts, the church wasn't growing. He comments:

> "So when the church continued to die a slow and painful death, I couldn't understand what God was doing ... He wasn't bringing people to the church. He wasn't helping me build a great church. And He sure wasn't concerned about my desire to be a successful pastor."[3]

It was in Pastor Barnett's moment of brokenness that the Lord clarified his mission. He learned what God actually had in mind. What he heard from the Lord was, "I did not bring you here to build a great church. I brought you here to build people—these people. You build the people, I'll build the church."[4] And so today, the Dream Center is a direct result of what Pastor Barnett pursued. He stopped pursuing his goal and began pursuing God's goal. Because he made his relationship with God a priority, he received clear instructions which are guiding him toward fulfilling his call today. He understood this Third Dimension—The Right Pursuit.

Paul's Encounter with Christ

The apostle Paul understood this Third Dimension of the call. How did he become so dynamic in his ministry? What made him and his crusade team so effective in spreading the gospel to the point that the Jews who opposed them complained that *they were the ones who turned the world upside down*? (see Acts 17:6) Was it his apostolic title alone? Was it wrapped up in his abilities, education, or background alone? The answer is no. The impact he made on the earth for the kingdom of God was a direct result of what he pursued.

In Acts 26:13–19, Paul stood trial before King Agrippa in Caesarea as a result of being accused by Jews that he was opposing Jewish law. As Paul defends himself, he begins to tell the king his story about his encounter with God on the road to Damascus and how he received his call from God. Based on his encounter, we can ascertain at least three things about the call on his life:

1. His Purpose – To become who God intended him to be—from Saul of Tarsus to the apostle Paul—and to be a witness to what God was about to reveal to him.
2. His Calling – To be a minister to the Gentile nation.
3. His Assignment – To open the eyes of those who were spiritually blind turn those people from darkness to the light. To be God's instrument so that people might receive forgiveness and their spiritual inheritance.

What Did He Pursue?

We know these were just the highlights of what God accomplished through the life of Paul. However, despite the incredible journey Paul was about to embark on, what was his primary pursuit? I believe it was eloquently stated in what I phrase as Paul's personal mission statement according to Philippians 3:10: *That I might know him.*

The word "know" in this verse means to have intimate knowledge of. Paul pursued a complete understanding of God through an intimate relationship with Jesus Christ. Jesus described true intimacy as being one, just as He was one with the Father (see John 17:11, 21–23).

Paul was interested in more than just God's power and wanted to know the Person behind the power. Paul took his relationship with Jesus beyond the Damascus road experience. Yes, he was saved from sin and was heaven bound, but he did not stop there. Paul went beyond the encounter and moved into discovery. The encounter was a single event, but discovery was an ongoing process of love and devotion.

My Encounter

I decided to go to church instead of watching TV again. It was a Saturday night, so going to church was different for me. I only went because the guys were going. I figured I'd rather hang out with someone doing something instead of being at home by myself doing nothing.

A nice crowd was at church that night. There were about 200 or so in attendance. Apparently, we were in a revival and there was a guest speaker. The pastor introduced our speaker for the night. I didn't mind, but I was ready to get through that part of the service, so the guys and I could hang out.

He stepped up to the pulpit. The choir stand was behind him, but the chairs were empty. Behind the choir stand was the baptismal pool and a cross that hung on the back wall. This cross was about four feet tall and about three feet wide. Lights illuminated it so that those in the back of the church could see the cross despite the distance.

WHAT DID PAUL PURSUE?

The speaker sang a couple of gospel songs right before he introduced the title of his message which was "Heaven and Hell." His introduction made me a little nervous. He first described the beauty of heaven. That was the lighter part of his message. When he began describing heaven's opposite, Hell, I got really nervous.

The minister started to get my attention. I endured the message, or at least I thought so. Then he turned out all the lights, and the only thing you could see was the cross hanging on the back wall of the church. As my attention focused on the lights behind the cross, the only light in the room, he said, "There's coming a time when those who don't give their hearts to Jesus will run out of time, and there will be no cross!"

Then he shut off the lights that were on the cross. The church was pitch dark. Needless to say, I was scared. As soon as they turned the house lights back on, I ran to the altar and gave my heart to Jesus!

Later, when my relationship with God was still new, I was kind of into God, yet I was still pursuing my own will. Whenever I got in trouble, I prayed. When I needed something, I prayed. I prayed when it was convenient for me. I seemed to always find myself crying out to God, repenting over the same mistakes and the same sins. I finally realized that I didn't have a sin issue but rather, a commitment issue. I had not totally surrendered my will to God.

Sadly, there are Christians who, after their born-again experience, stop at the cross of Calvary. They experience an encounter with God but never go beyond that initial transformation. They are satisfied with attending church maybe once or twice a week and experience God through praise and worship or through teaching or preaching, but the extent of their relationship with God is a Sunday morning experience. They are content with only praying to

God out of convenience, to have Him meet their needs or aid them when they are in trouble. But this isn't how God wants us to live. Like Paul, every believer should be turning this world upside down. We should be reigning in this life, not merely existing. Paul had a greater testimony about who Christ was because he plunged into pursuing Him.

Laying Hold

> Not that I have already attained, or am already perfected; but I press on, that I may lay hold of that for which Christ Jesus has also laid hold of me.
> —Philippians 3:12 NKJV

As a child growing up, we lived in the country, about an hour's drive outside of L.A. My favorite thing was to run around barefoot, and that's just what I did. Wearing shoes was for special occasions, like going to church or school. We lived near our cousins so there were plenty of kids to play with. I remember in the middle of the day, playing one of our favorite games, Hide and Seek. We all hid, as one of the cousins we considered to be "it" had to lean on part of the house (we called the base) with eyes closed, counting to ten. While counting, those of us who were not "it" would go hid in our favorite places: behind our aunt's bushes, under the house, or in our neighbor's backyard. We'd hide anywhere we thought wouldn't be seen. If you could return back to the base without being tagged by the person who was "it," you were good. But if you were tagged, you had to be "it" for the next round.

Sure enough during one particular day playing the game, as soon as my cousin disappeared to look for us, I made a mad dash to the base. I thought, "If I can get there before I'm tagged, then I'm good." I ran as fast as I could, when all of a sudden, I felt this excruciating pain!

"Oh God!" I cried out.

Suddenly, I went leaping into the air, grabbing my foot while twisting and turning before landing on the ground. And here comes the unfortunate part of being barefoot: I was just stung by a bee that became stuck between my toes! At that moment, running toward the base wasn't so important anymore. For me the game came to a screeching halt. Of course, I still got tagged. I was "it," but it didn't matter. All I knew was that I was trying to lay hold of that bee that laid hold of me.

Jesus got a hold of Paul on that road to Damascus like that bee got a hold of me. In return, Paul emphasized that he was trying to get a hold of that which laid hold of him. Paul's experience of God is evident as we read the New Testament. And yet, he emphasizes in Philippians 3:12 that he has not arrived nor was he at such a spiritual maturity "beyond which there is no progress, but I am pursuing onward."[5] He had to grasp, understand, and comprehend every aspect of the Person of Jesus Christ. His intimate knowledge of God and rich relationship were a direct result of what he pursued: to know Christ. This pursuit was his priority.

Shared Experiences

Secondly, Paul gained an intimate knowledge and understanding of Christ, through what I call, "shared experiences." Paul said that he wanted to know Christ "in an experiential way, and come to know experientially the power of His resurrection and the joint-participation in His sufferings."[6] So Paul wanted shared experiences with Christ in two ways: in glory and in suffering.

In our marriage, my wife and I have shared both the good and the bad. Some good highlights include our dates, vacations, buying our first house, and raising kids. I'd say this represents the glory aspect of our marriage. But then there's been the suffering side: the birth of our kids (of course she suffered more than I did), sickness, job loss, kids' conflicts in school, trips to the hospital, disagreements, etc. These are just examples of our shared experiences. It was through these shared experiences that we learned about each other, began to understand each other, and started to communicate at a deeper level. We've come to appreciate each other's uniqueness. Our shared experiences create greater intimacy.

Pastor Barnett of the Dream Center described a particular experience of when he decided to see what it would be like to have no money, to beg, to survive the night, and endure the streets of Los Angeles, just so he could relate and better understand the suffering of those who don't have alternative options. He explained why:

> "I am the pastor of a mega church, a proud bastion of Christianity in the heart of downtown Los Angeles. Tonight was the fifteenth anniversary of the beginning of our ministry, known as the Dream Center ... I decided this was where I wanted to spend that anniversary, living among the very people I have come to love during these past fifteen years ... to dig more deeply into their world so I could serve them more profoundly."[7]

Paul emphasized that it's through our shared experience with Christ that we really come to know Him. Not only will we *encounter* "Who" God is, but also, we'll *experience* "Who" God is.

God's Glory

When God manifests Himself in a tangible way, His glory is on display. God's glory was revealed as He unfolded layer upon layer of revelations to Paul, concerning the mystery of Christ (Ephesians 3:3, 17–20). It's evident God's glory was revealed through Paul's writing of most of the New Testament, as the Holy Spirit inspired him. Paul revealed God's glory by establishing the Gentile churches. God's glory manifested and the church grew and matured as a result of Paul's teaching and his obedience to the call. Paul shared in the glory.

With the glory comes suffering, and Paul definitely shared in Christ's suffering. Glory and suffering go together like a two-sided coin. Paul wanted to understand more than just the sufferings of Christ. He also wanted to know what it meant to suffer with Him. He revealed a little of what he had endured for the sake of Christ. He had been beaten, imprisoned, robbed, shipwrecked, and stoned. He had gone without food and water, had been stranded and had been homeless at times. He had experienced pain from all angles—physical and emotional. He had endured persecution, peril, and a life of inconveniences, just to preach the gospel (2 Corinthians 11:23–28). But through it all, he learned that no tribulation, distress, persecution, famine, peril, or sword could separate him from God's love for him and his love for God (Romans 8:35–37).

Paul became convinced of God's love through his shared experiences with God. This is how we really come to know Him as Christ. As we share in the sufferings of Christ, it helps us to focus on what's most important. We'll experience God in tangible ways and His Word in such a way that it becomes more than just words written on a page. God is ready to make known His power to us, especially in our time of need.

What Will It Cost Me?

> But whatever was to my profit I now consider loss for the sake of Christ. What is more, I consider everything a loss

compared to the surpassing greatness of knowing Christ Jesus my Lord, for whose sake I have lost all things. I consider them rubbish, that I may gain Christ.
—Philippians 3:7–8 NIV

One Sunday my pastor encouraged us to go on a fast. I went to him after service and asked how I could fast without losing weight. At that time, I was young, right out of high school, attending junior college, and my focus was on gaining weight. I was exercising, lifting weights, and drinking lots of protein drinks. My goal was to bulk up so I could feel better about how I looked. Of course, I wouldn't have admitted that back then, but that was reality. I will never forget the response my pastor gave me.

"Do you know what your problem is?"

"No sir, what is it?"

"You're not willing to make a sacrifice."

"Yes sir, yes I am."

But as I walked away, I realized he was right. What personal sacrifices was I willing to make in order to gain another experience with Christ? I had to set aside my blinding ambitions and be willing to decrease so God could increase in me. What was I willing to give up for the sake of experiencing more of God?

In Genesis 22, Abraham was ready to sacrifice his son Isaac on the altar. That is when he experienced God as Jehovah Jireh, his Provider; a side of God he hadn't experienced until that moment. When you are willing to make personal sacrifices for God, you have the opportunity to experience a side of God that you may have never seen before.

Counting as Loss

Paul was so committed to his pursuit of Christ that he was even willing to give up the things he used to his advantage. He stated in Philippians 3:7, "But what things were gain to me, these I have counted loss for Christ."[8] What were the things that were gains? In verses 4–6, he talks about his achievements, his heritage, and his past. How we relate to these three things can impact our moving from encounter to discovery with Christ.

First, Paul was ready to deny his achievements. Achievements refer to his goals and ambitions in life. Concerning the law, Paul was blameless. He dotted every "I" and crossed every "t" when it came to keeping the law. As a Pharisee, he was at the top of the religious charts. He had such a zeal for the law that he persecuted all those who opposed it. He upheld his religious beliefs at any cost. Paul showed us that he was willing to lay it all down. He said, "But all these things that I once thought very worthwhile, now I've thrown them all away."[9] This was total self-denial. He counted as a loss to the detriment of his flesh, his ego, and his independent thinking.

Imagine you're preparing for a job interview. Your resume is printed and ready to present to the interviewer, but right before the interview, you take an eraser and erase all your job history, skills, and educational achievements. You also don't talk about it during your interview because you've counted it all as loss. That may seem a bit extreme, but Paul's mentality was such that he was willing to let go of what he gained so it would not hinder his pursuit for Christ. His attitude was that no matter how God blessed yesterday, each day was a new day, and he needed more of Him for the present day.

Secondly, Paul was willing to deny his heritage—the things he had going for him. He was from the tribe of Benjamin. He was a true Hebrew. He could have used this heritage as an advantage. Today, this equates to having social, cultural, or even financial status. And sometimes as

Christians, we let our status and positions get in the way of our obedience. We have to step out of our comfort zones. There are times God is calling us to greater challenges, but to answer that call, we must be willing to let go of where we are and what we have today, and we must also be willing to let go of the third item on Paul's list—the past.

Through shared experiences with Christ, Paul learned to forget the past. He stated in verse 13, "I am still not all I should be, but I am bringing all my energies to bear on this one thing: Forgetting the past and looking forward to what lies ahead."[10] Sometimes, it's hard to let go of how things used to be or those who have hurt you. Paul was depending on Christ's strength to get him through to the future God had for him (see 2 Corinthians 12:9). We are encouraged to do the same, but we must be willing.

I have heard people say, "I'll forgive, but I won't forget." Keep in mind, to forgive is to let something go, which implies you are willing to release it. Paul was able to release his past by forgetting, but not forgetting in the sense that negative experiences were erased from his memory. What Paul meant by forgetting was that the sting of that event was gone; the pain had been anesthetized by God's grace. So his past could not negatively influence his future.

Remember what I shared earlier about being stung by a bee between my toes? The bee didn't like being stepped on any more than I enjoyed the discomfort of being stung. The pain between my toes was agonizing. Unfortunately, after the initial sting, the stinger was still there, lodged between my toes. So, I had to remove the stinger for the relief and healing process to start. In my mind, my foot started to immediately feel better, but in reality, it took a few days for the healing process to be completed.

The inner healing of the heart process takes place when we, like Paul, are willing to forgive and forget. The decision to forgive from the heart is like removing the stinger. Once we forgive, God's grace will anesthetize the pain. He removes the sting of the event and heals the wound in our hearts. Then to complete the healing process, God will help us forget. He removes the ability of that hurt to influence or hinder our future in a negative way, all because we are willing to release the past. What was behind Paul, was behind him. What's behind you, is behind you.

That I Might Win

Paul was determined to win not just any prize. The prize was Christ. He emphasized, "Yea doubtless, and I count all things but loss for the excellency of the knowledge of Christ Jesus my Lord: for whom I have suffered the loss of all things, and do count them but dung, that I may win Christ."[11]

Paul pressed toward the prize of winning Christ with uninterrupted focus, in spite of himself. Paul described his own struggles with his flesh as a warring against the law of God (see Romans 7). And yet, to gain another experience with Christ, Paul would not allow his carnal nature to get in his way. He reckoned his accomplishments, his heritage, and even his past as dung, in order to move closer to God. Just as he was challenged, we are challenged today.

God can take all that we have experienced, the positive and negative, and make it all work for our good. However, should our heritage, our past history, our accomplishments, and even our failures become a hindrance to our primary pursuit, we must consider them all as useless. We must reject and despise anything that gets in the way of our authentic worship and commitment to God.

When you think you have arrived, you are in the way. When you get to the place where you can't learn anymore, you are in the way. When you get to the place where obtaining God's daily instructions for your life is not a priority, then you are in the way. If your past hinders you from moving forward, then you are in the way. You have to consider it all as dung. Like with Paul, every day was a new day, and he looked forward to a new experience with Christ. We cannot allow what we accomplished yesterday to hinder our opportunity to gain a new experience with Christ today.

Paul's attitude said, "I have written another letter, I have established another church, I have received new vision and new revelation of the mystery of Christ, but today is a new day, and on today, what matters is doing what it takes to win another experience with Christ."

To win something, you must go after it until you have obtained it. At every level of obedience, you give up a part of yourself to win another experience with Christ. Paul recognized that there was more to God yet to be discovered. He described the vastness of the person of Jesus Christ as unsearchable riches having incredible depth, height, length, and width. In other words, you will never reach the end of Christ's riches—the point of full comprehension. And you will never get to the point where you have arrived because the thirst and hunger for God is never ending. Understanding the importance of the right pursuit aligns us in position to fulfill this next dimension—Understanding Our Role.

Chapter 6
7 Principles

1. Paul took his relationship with Jesus beyond the road of Damascus experience. Paul went beyond the encounter into discovery. The encounter was a single event, but discovery was an ongoing process.

2. Paul emphasized that it's through our shared experience with Christ that we really come to know Him. Not only will we encounter who God is, but also, we'll experience who God is.

3. When you are willing to make personal sacrifices for God, you have the opportunity to experience a side of God that you may have never seen before.

4. Making the decision to forgive from the heart is like removing the stinger. Forgiveness allows God's grace to anesthetize the pain. He removes the sting of the event from our wounded hearts.

5. To gain another experience with Christ, Paul would not allow his carnal nature to get in his way. He reckoned his accomplishments, his heritage, and even his past as dung, in order to move closer to God.

6. We cannot allow what we accomplished yesterday to hinder our opportunity to gain a new experience with Christ today.

7. At every level of obedience, we give up a part of ourselves to win another experience with Christ.

THE FOURTH DIMENSION: UNDERSTANDING OUR ROLE

CHAPTER 7

THE CALL DEFINES US

> Paul, called to be an apostle of Jesus Christ through the will of God, and Sosthenes our brother.
> —1 Corinthians 1:1 KJV

I PULLED UP in the parking lot after several minutes of searching. All I had to do was drop off some lunch to a family friend of ours. I felt like an errand boy, but that didn't bother me much because I was in the "zone." I was excited—fresh out of college with a job, a car, and a new sense of freedom. Although I moved back home with my parents initially, I was only there temporarily. A few days of fun remained before I had to report to my first day of work at my new job. I thought, *As soon as I start working and making some money, I can declare that I am fully independent, and on my way. I'm going to travel, eat what I want, buy clothes, hang out with my friends, and actually afford to go out on a date. Can't wait to be my own man!*

My thoughts had carried me up the concrete steps and into a storefront building. The beauty parlor was packed and busy. There were ladies everywhere: some sitting under the hair dryers, others laid back on their chairs, getting their hair washed, and still others getting their nails done. Conversations and noise galore filled the air. The chemical aroma of a perm and the scent of sweetness from shampoo and conditioner floated through the room. I looked around and spotted my friend standing at the cash register and having a conversation with the woman I believed to be the owner of the shop. As soon as I walked in, conversations died to a dull roar and all eyes focused on me. My friend and I greeted each other as casually as possible, and then I handed her lunch to her. When she introduced me to her boss, immediately, the woman's eyes locked on me. Before I could react, I heard familiar words again, but this time, they came from a total stranger.

"You're a preacher, aren't you?"

"No, I'm not," I responded.

"Yes you are. You're a preacher."

"No, I'm not."

"Child, I know a minister when I see one, and you're one."

"Sorry ma'am, but you're wrong! For the last time, I'm not a preacher!"

Finally, my friend jumped in. She could tell I was frustrated with the conversation.

"Betty, leave him alone." She attempted to empathize with me. "He's trying to do a good deed, but there you go bein' busy!"

Immediately, I was out the door! I didn't want to hear anymore.

It was like I had a stamp on my forehead and a neon sign on my back that said, "Minister." I was single, fresh out of college, and all I wanted to do was have some fun, but God was calling me to so much more than what I envisioned for my own life. Though the calling was irrefutable, my denial was intentional. As a result, I stayed frustrated, marking time.

I wondered if Jonah felt the same way on board that ship headed to Tarshish when God sent the storm. Jonah had to come to grips with the reality that he was the reason for the storm. I too had to accept that the source of my frustration was my own doing. I was running from God; trying to find myself outside of what God was calling me to do. How many people was I impacting through my denial and disobedience to what God summoned me to? What you are, is part of who you are. So to trying to fill roles outside of what you are will only lead to frustration for yourself and for others. What I've come to learn is that your calling defines you. Your calling is like purpose; it's something you're born with. You can't push it away; you just have to fulfill it.

The Call Defines What You Are

In the previous chapters, we recognized that God defines who we are. How effective we are for the kingdom of God is based on our relationship with God and not merely on our gifts and talents. Now that we've established the proper foundation, we can move on to this Fourth Dimension of the call—Understanding Our Role.

Romans 12:4 says that even though there are many in the body of Christ, all "do not have the same office." Office here is translated as the word function, which means role or position. Paul described his role in Romans 1:1, saying he is "a servant of Christ Jesus, called to be an apostle and set apart for the gospel of God."[1] This word "called" is translated as "appointed," which means that God designated Paul to fill this position.[2]

Additionally, Paul was made an apostle by divine summons.[3] The summons shaped Paul into the apostle he needed to be. This is where the call (the summons) on your life shapes the calling (the role).

Authors Graves, Addington, and Womack wrote the book, *Cornerstones for Calling*. The text further defines calling as "God's personal invitation for me to work on His agenda. And how I can use the talents He has given me in ways that are eternally significant."[4]

This phase of the call on our lives defines the type of conduit by which the power of the Holy Spirit is unleashed. Just as electricity has to be governed and managed, this stage of our call governs how the gifts and talents that God equipped us with, are used. This level of our call determines how the Holy Spirit will work in our lives and how we fit into God purposes. It defines our function or role in the body of Christ, which explains why we have gifts and talents in the first place. I'm referring to this dimension of our call as one that defines "what" we are rather than "who" we are.

Here are a few ways God can reveal your calling:

1. You may discover your calling by a direct encounter with God. God spoke to Moses from a burning bush and tasked him with delivering Israel from Egypt's oppression. Paul discovered his calling by direct encounter with Jesus on the road to Damascus.
2. God can give you a strong sense of purpose to reveal your calling. Dr. Miles Munroe, author of, *In Pursuit of Purpose*, asserts that, "God never requires anything of His creation that He didn't already build into them."[5] There are some things you are naturally good at or that capture your attention. What do you naturally gravitate to? That which captures

your attention could be an indicator of where your calling leads.
3. A burden to see specific change in your environment can be an indicator of your calling. Nehemiah is a good example. When Nehemiah heard about the condition of Jerusalem, how the walls were destroyed, and the city was burned with fire, he wept. He had a burning desire to see the walls of Jerusalem restored. Nehemiah said, "So it was, when I heard these words, that I sat down and wept, and mourned for many days; I was fasting and praying before the God of heaven" (Nehemiah 1:4).
4. God can use a burning passion to bring you into your calling. Mike Murdock said, "You will only have significant success with something that is an obsession ... if what you love begins to consume your mind, your thoughts, your conversation, your schedule, look for extraordinary success."[6] We saw David's passion for God through his worship. He stated in Psalm 69:9, "My zeal for God and his work burns hot within me. And because I advocate your cause, your enemies insult me even as they insult you."[7] God used him to re-establish authentic worship in the earth. What are you passionate about? What do you love to do? Rick Warren said, "When you are doing what you love to do, no one has to motivate you."[8]
5. God can speak directly through His Word to lead you into your calling. Dr. Ron Deberry, Academic Dean for Bethel College, describes his experience this way, "I can relate back to when I got saved ... I wasn't saved for more than 5–6 months when I was studying the word of God and the Spirit of God led me to Matthew 9:37–38 that says, 'the harvest

is plentiful but the labors are few.' God captured my heart ... that's when I knew He called me for a purpose and He had a plan for my life."[9]
6. The needs of others that you enjoy meeting can be an indicator to your calling. What problem in the world, in your community, or around you do you feel compelled to solve? What needs in others' lives get your attention? Gordon Smith emphasized that callings are always an element of how we perceive the "brokenness of the world."[10] Fredrick Buechner emphasized, "The place God calls you is the place where your deep gladness and the world's deep hunger meet."[11]

God can speak through a dream or a vision to reveal your calling. He can even use pain and suffering as your motivator. He can use the things that anger or frustrate you the most to prompt you toward your calling.

These are just a few examples. God is not limited in how He chooses to reveal your calling to you. The key is to recognize when you sense the summons and take steps toward realizing and fulfilling it.

Vocations Divinely Inspired

Some are called to ministry. Jesus called the twelve one by one. He transformed their vocations from secular to ministry, i.e. Peter the fisherman and Luke the physician were changed into ministers of the Gospel. God calls people to specific leadership roles as spiritual vocations in the body of Christ for the purpose of equipping believers to do the work of ministry (see Ephesians 4:11–12). However, if you're not called to one of these roles, it doesn't mean there isn't a calling on your life.

God call's some into secular vocations as ministry, i.e. attorneys, school teachers, scientists, doctors, etc. Os Guinness, author of, *The Call*, highlighted a man named William Wilberforce, who is an example of one called into a secular vocation rather than church as ministry, in the late 1700's. God used Wilberforce as a politician to abolish slave trading in the British Empire. Slave trading was the mainstream of the British economy at the time. Despite the odds against him, God called Wilberforce to "champion the liberty of the oppressed—as a Parliamentarian."[12]

God calls us to all arenas of life. Wherever there are lost and hurting people who need the Gospel, God calls us to minister. In the book, *Courage & Calling*, Gordon T. Smith affirmed, "The sacred is not distinct from the secular; rather the sacred is what sanctifies the ordinary and thus makes it good & noble."[13]

Os Guinness also asserts, "The businessman, teacher, factory worker can do God's work or fail to do God's work just as much as minister or missionary."[14] Whatever the role God has for you—in church, the mission field, a Fortune 500 company or business owner—can be divinely inspired. Even though some of us don't have the title of pastor, bishop, or evangelist, or work in full-time ministry, we have to remember it's all about how God wants to use us to enrich the lives of others.

Training Ground

God chooses your training ground to prepare you for work in the kingdom. God can use the secular workplace as the training ground. God used shepherding sheep as the workplace for David, before God called him to Shepherd His people Israel. Joseph's training ground was not in the church per se, but rather, in the secular workplace

(Egypt). God used Potiphar to develop Joseph's gifts in administration and organization. God used slavery and prison to cultivate a compassionate heart in Joseph. He even used life's circumstances and Joseph's experience with his brothers. God can use anything and any place to prepare you for your calling.

Paul, a tent maker by trade, provided physical covering for anyone who needed it, but later as an apostle, he provided spiritual covering for God's people (see Acts 18:1–3). His tool of trade helped prepare him for his spiritual vocation in the Kingdom of God.

Also note that your secular vocation may change, but your calling is divine and is always permanent. Why? Because God said something about you before you were born. Luke was a physician before he was called to be a fellow laborer with the apostle Paul, and the author of two New Testament books—the Gospel of Luke and the Book of Acts.[15] His natural vocation changed, but the call on his life was permanent because God called him before the foundations of the earth (see Ephesians 2:10).

Processing the Call

So how do I begin to process and walk out what I feel God is saying? One way is by serving others. Serving others helps to clarify your calling. Pastor Matthew Barnett, author of, *The Cause within You*, said, "Don't sit around doing nothing, waiting for the perfect circumstances to bring clarity ... If you're trying to figure out what God created you to do, just roll up your sleeves and start serving in cooperation with somebody else's cause."[16]

The discovery of one's calling can be immediate or may unfold over time. I know beyond a shadow of a doubt that God called me to be an author. However, in other areas of my life, God has been revealing deeper aspects of my calling over time. As I act on what I know, God reveals more. Remember, the calling is not a destination; it's a journey. It's not a finite event but a process.

Going through the process allows you to discover more about your calling by bridging the gap. Professor David Trickett, President of Iliff School of Theology, encourages those who are searching for their calling,

> "To identify their story and look at the gap between their yearnings and their experiences. And suggest that the path to fulfilling calling is actually a menu that consists of working on the gap between what it is we yearn to do and be and what we are currently doing and being."[17]

As you follow God on this journey of bridging this gap, you will find that the calling is bigger and broader than you realize, which requires that you have an open mind. There is no threshold to what you can accomplish for God. One way to keep an open mind so that you don't limit God is by exposure. Pastor Glenn Reynolds of Bethel Church asserts:

> "Exposure creates the climate for the call to be able to happen; to stretch our minds because it's hard to be called to something that we've not been exposed to. Obviously, in the bible God called people to do things they had no clue about—go build an Ark, and there never had been an Ark, but at the same time, there has to be some sense of exposure because God works within who we are and what we've seen to bring about something out of our minds into reality. The key is to not put God in a box but to expose ourselves to all kinds of things whether its mission trips, meeting people, reading books, traveling, conferences, etc. … it's important to get out of our small world because a different place, a different pace gives a

different perspective. God can speak to us in different ways. I just think the call can be broader than we imagine, rather than this is what I'm called to forever, we might as well say; I'm called to obey, called to be faithful."[18]

God called Jesus to be the Savior of the world, and yet, that encompassed many different things, such as, healer, teacher, miracle worker, and sacrificial lamb, just to name a few. For Jesus, the volumes of books written about Him couldn't contain all that He accomplished. Our callings are so vast that it will take a lifetime to discover the fullness of what God has said about each of us. Now let's explore the distinct elements of a calling.

Components of Your Calling

While in college, I ran across an associate with whom I attended high school. He was employed at the college, and every so often, we would cross paths and talk about our goals in life. One day, he made a statement that shocked me. He felt like the education field that he chose to pursue was the wrong field because his salary wasn't big enough, so he was considering an alternative vocation.

Instead of teaching, this man's top alternative choice was to be a pastor of a large, denominational church. I was shocked because his primary reason for wanting to be a pastor was not because he sensed a calling, but rather, because he believed he could make more money doing so. He was in for a rude awakening.

There are four distinct components pertaining to your calling. The first component relates to what I shared in chapter 1. The call is a distinct appointment. This means that God chooses. God sent the prophet Samuel to anoint David as the next king over Israel, after He rejected Saul, Israel's first king. God told the prophet Samuel to go anoint the one "whom I have named" (see 1 Samuel 16:3, 13). In First Corinthians 1:1, Paul explained that he was called as an apostle by the will of God. This proves that in the kingdom of God, a calling is more than a title on a business card; it's a sovereign determination.

The second component of your calling is that it has a distinct authority. My wife and I attended a special service one evening at a local ministry. This event drew a pretty large crowd. At the end, a police car pulled into the parking lot. An officer stepped out of the car, put on a bright yellow reflective jacket, and walked right onto the main street. Meanwhile, cars were racing forty plus miles per hour, headed her way. The officer positioned herself right under the traffic light, which was green by the way, favoring the cars headed toward her. Then, with her left hand, she held her whistle and blew it, and with her right hand, she motioned the oncoming traffic to stop!

The fast-approaching traffic came to a screeching halt. Then she turned toward the long line of cars waiting to exit the church parking lot and motioned us to go. We pulled out into the traffic and proceeded home.

This policewoman understood her authority and exercised it. The oncoming traffic recognized her authority as well because they came to an immediate stop. According to Ephesians 4:7, we all have been given God's grace "according to the measure of the gift of Christ." The measure of Christ refers to our measure of authority.

Paul's measure of Christ or authority was an apostolic authority. God gave him authority to establish the New Testament church among the Gentiles. Like the police officer who commanded the traffic to halt, the God of heaven has authorized you for your calling. And when God delegates authority, it's recognized in three dimensions.

1. Our authority is recognized in Heaven. In Acts 26:16, God tells Paul, "For this purpose I appeared unto thee." Paul responded to the call and summed it up in 1 Corinthians 1:1 that it was God's will. In other words, he acknowledged that his apostleship was authorized by Heaven.
2. Our authority is recognized on earth. Paul was recognized as one of the greatest apostles. He walked in this apostolic authority. As we read the New Testament, we can tell that God had put a word in Paul's spirit. The New Testament reflects the fruits of his apostolic authority.
3. Our authority is recognized under the earth. Paul's apostolic authority was recognized by the kingdom of darkness. Acts 19 reports how God used Paul in performing miracles. Then a group of men called the seven sons of Sceva tried to imitate Paul by trying to cast out a demon spirit. To those sons of Sceva, the evil spirit responded, "Jesus I know, and Paul I know; but who are you?" (Acts 19:15) When you are fulfilling your calling, you are a threat to the kingdom of darkness.

The third component of your call is that there is a distinct anointing. God anoints you for service and consecrates you to the office or position to which you're called. In other words, God anoints you to be "what" you are. In Exodus, we see Aaron was consecrated to minister to the Lord in the priest's office. So this distinct anointing consecrates us for the position that our calling requires.

A Part of the Whole

Just as there are many parts to our bodies, so it is with Christ's body. We are all parts of it, and it takes every

one of us to make it complete, for we each have different work to do. So we belong to each other, and each needs all the others.
—Romans 12:4 TLB

The final component of the calling is that you have a distinct position in the body of Christ. In the book of Romans, Paul compares the body of Christ to the natural body. He uses this analogy to explain some important truths about how essential we are to God's program. He begins by illustrating how the human body has multiple parts that make up the whole body. Every believer is part of and contributes to the bigger entity—the body of Christ. In 1 Corinthians 12:18, Paul affirms, "But now God has set the members, each one of them, in the body just as He pleased."[19] The word "members" literally means limbs. In the same way in which our fingers are connected to our hands, which are connected to our arms, which are connected to our shoulders, and so on, God has set us in our position and determined how we would connect in the body of Christ. With this continuous connection comes dependencies; each part must work in synchronization with the other parts to maintain harmony and balance. We are therefore interdependent, meaning we need each other.

Each Part Is Independent

Each interdependent part works separately and independently of each other. Each part has a specific function. The eyes are distinct from the ears. The feet are distinct from the hands. The eye is for vision, and the ear is to hear. And yet all parts when functioning together, benefit the whole body.

Furthermore, every part of the human body does something exclusive, and no two parts are exactly the same.

Now, I realize that you have two hands, so you may think, "that's not one of a kind." But think of about it, how many left hands do you have? Your hands are similar but are not exactly the same. Every fingerprint is unique and so is each strand of hair. You are unique, and you play an exclusive role in the body. Your role may be similar to another, but it is not exactly the same. You are called to be a blessing. Your personality, your gifts, your ways of doing things can touch a life in ways that the person right next to you doing a similar thing may not be able to accomplish.

You Have a Place

God has put us where He wants us; whether sacred or secular, ordinary or divine, or even a combination of both. There's room for each of us in God's orchestra.

Years ago, I frequently visited a particular church that was well known for its conferences and guest speakers. This church had quite a number of gifted musicians on staff and serving as volunteers. Being a musician myself, I knew many of them personally. Unfortunately, many of these overflow musicians seemed to be waiting on their opportunity to serve, but for many of them, the opportunity never came. Meanwhile, other churches in the area needed musicians to help them grow their ministries so they could carry out what God called them to do, yet these very capable musicians weren't interested in playing at these smaller churches. Remember, there is enough room for you in God's program. God has carved out a place for you.

Significance

In the reality TV series called, *Undercover Boss*, a member of a company's senior management team (like the president, CEO, or owner of the company) disguises himself or herself as an everyday employee. In the disguise, the "boss" works alongside the employee in the field or production area. The goal is for management to experience a day in the life of an employee and to learn more about the company from the employees' perspective.

In one particular episode, the president of a college had to cut their college budget, which had adverse effects on various school programs. In particular, the president wanted to know the impact on their agricultural operations, so he went undercover and disguised himself as an hourly field worker.

The undercover president worked alongside a greenhouse technician, cleaning greenhouses in order to learn this technician's job. There were acres of greenhouses, which stored thousands of plants involved in research. One of the technician's tasks was to paint pieces of wood with a special chemical solution used to prevent viruses from moving from one plant to another. The president stated, "If not done correctly, a student's or faculty member's research could get different or bad results and nobody would ever know why."

What he recognized about that technician was "that he wasn't just painting stuff but rather was being a piece of a much larger research project and improving our knowledge base about plants." He understood that the quality of their research could impact their reputation and future funding.

The technician explained how he wrote letters and offered suggestions to the president's office but he felt no one listened. This technician felt insignificant.

At the end of their conversation, the president revealed himself to the technician. That day, he recognized the value this employee brought to the college and others like him and how important it was for employees to be heard.

This technician's seemingly insignificant role made a very positive impact toward the future of that college. In his role, he helped to serve and protect the credibility of their agricultural division and ultimately other communities.[20]

> If the foot says, "I am not a part of the body because I am not a hand," that does not make it any less a part of the body. And what would you think if you heard an ear say, "I am not part of the body because I am only an ear and not an eye"? Would that make it any less a part of the body?
>
> Suppose the whole body were an eye—then how would you hear? Or if your whole body were just one big ear, how could you smell anything? But that isn't the way God has made us. He has made many parts for our bodies and has put each part just where he wants it.
> —1 Corinthians 12:15–18 TLB

Here in First Corinthians, Paul points out that no matter how significant or insignificant you may perceive your role to be, your part is important to God's work. Many times, we undervalue our roles when we compare ourselves to others. Which role was more important for that college—the president's or the greenhouse technician's? They both were because less responsibility doesn't mean less significance. First Corinthians 12:22 reads, "And some of the parts that seem weakest and least important are really the most necessary."[21] If God created the role, then it's necessary.

How can a company run successfully without the president, the visionary? Most likely, there would be no company without that person. However, how can a company run if pipes are clogged or the trash never gets dumped? Even a restaurant with the most creative chef would not get very far in impressing hungry people willing to pay a premium price for their meals, if there were no dishwasher or busboy present. In God's kingdom no matter what your role is, it's valuable because He made it.

Not Visible Doesn't Mean It's Not Valuable

Additionally, even if your role is not visible, that doesn't mean it's not valuable. We recognize the eyes and nose as visible parts of the body, but what about the internal workings of the human body? Just because you don't see your heart or liver, does that mean they are not necessary or less valuable? How about the tonsils? You can't see them like you see your eyes and ears, but they're still important to the work of your body.

The tonsils, which are positioned at the entrance of the throat, guard the body against bacteria, viruses, and other possible infections. One expert described the tonsils as "soldiers fighting on the boarder who get injured (inflamed) protecting the country."[22] Despite controversy in the medical profession about their value, some experts have concluded that the tonsils are still vital to the body's natural self-defense.

This illustration stands to reason that no matter how small you perceive your role in the body of Christ, whether you're in the forefront or behind the scenes like the tonsils, your role has purpose and is vital to promoting the health of the Church and important to the work of God.

Working Properly

God equipped each of us with skills to aid each other. However, in order for each part to work properly, unity is required, just like in the human body. For example, built within each human body is the ability to heal itself. When there is an illness or ailment, the body unifies as it goes into a self-healing mode. When there is a virus present, the body uses a fever to burn out the infection. The body turns a deep cut into a scab, then eventually into a scar. When we are in our places and in unity, we cause healthy growth in the body of Christ (see Ephesians 4:16). Each part supplies the other parts as we allow God's love and healing to flow through us to others.

We don't have to be perfect to get involved in the kingdom of God. Working properly doesn't mean that God doesn't still have work to do in us.(I believe what the Psalmist said about how the Holy Spirit will perfect the things that concern us in Psalm 138:8).

Ecclesiastes 11:4 says, "If you wait for perfect conditions, you will never get anything done."[23] So if you're waiting until you can practice more, study more, get a degree, or find more time, you might miss out. Start with what you have and where you are. As you faithfully sow what you have, God will increase you, and the body of Christ benefits. This means that to grow in God, you have to be in position to supply, actively allowing God to work in you "to will and do of His good pleasure." If you notice a part of the body of Christ that is lacking, could it be the position is waiting on you, a joint to supply the demand? Therefore be what God has called you to be.

Chapter 7

7 Principles

1. Your calling defines you. It likes purpose. It's something you're born with. You can't push it away; you just have to fulfill it.

2. Your secular vocation may change, but your calling is divine and always permanent.

3. In the kingdom of God, a calling is more than a title on a business card; It's a sovereign determination.

4. God set you in your position in the body of Christ based on what pleased Him.

5. Your personality, your gifts, and your ways of doing things can touch a life in ways that the person right next to you, doing a similar thing, may not be able to accomplish.

6. Even if your role is not visible, it doesn't mean it's not valuable.

7. If you notice a part of the body of Christ that is lacking, could it be the position is waiting on you, a joint to supply the demand?

CHAPTER 8

FINDING OUR PLACE

> Under his direction, the whole body is fitted together perfectly.
> —Ephesians 4:16 NLT

I PULLED INTO the parking lot of the restaurant where we all agreed to meet, but I didn't realize that I had arrived so soon. I'd just left my job interview. I had to make a decision soon, because I was in my senior year with only a semester to go before I graduated from college. This was about the tenth company with which I had interviewed, and their job offer made number three. This time, the company was an auditing firm in Dallas, Texas.

"Take your time thinking about it," the HR director had told me. "You have until March to let us know."

That was just a couple of months away. Now I had to decide if I wanted to work in Dallas, Houston, or Atlanta. As long as I didn't take a job anywhere in Oklahoma, I thought my decision shouldn't be that difficult. I was determined not to move back to my home town. But for some reason, even though I was excited on the outside, I didn't feel the same way on the inside.

When I stepped out of the car, my first thought was, *Hum, this is an odd looking restaurant.* But I was too preoccupied with contemplating my decision to really take notice of where I was, but it didn't matter. I was told this place was an "all you can eat" diner, so that was good enough for me. I was going to enjoy myself.

I was meeting up with some college peers from the area, and I was the guest in town. Upon entering, the waiter directed us to our seats. While walking, I began to feel a bit uncomfortable, though I was unsure why. I pushed the feeling aside. After all, the table was spread, and an amazing smorgasbord of food lay before us: deli meats, chicken wings, meat balls, and all types of buns and rolls. All you could eat for only a dollar. Wow! What a deal.

While I was stuffing my mouth with the entrees, I finally noticed the room was kind of dark, even though it was a sunny afternoon. There was music, and to my surprise, some people jumped onto a dance floor. Then I noticed across the room from where we were seated, people were ordering drinks from a bar. *A bar!* I thought. Then it dawned on me. This wasn't a restaurant; it was a club!

Right at that moment, I heard the Spirit of God say, "If you move away from where I want you, this will be your life. You will miss your calling!"

Suddenly I felt alone in the crowded room. I sensed God's presence, but it was more of a grieving sensation, as if God was moving on, and I was being left behind. I began to realize that God didn't want me in Dallas, Houston, or Atlanta. He had plans for me back home in Tulsa. I had a choice to make—follow God or go my own way and circumvent His plan for my life.

As I returned to school to finish out my last semester, I continued to hold on to those three offer letters, but I had no peace. I knew if I accepted any of those offers, I would veer off the path God had for me. Over the next several weeks, I continued to deliberate over my decision. I thought, *If I turn down these jobs, I may end up with nothing, but I have to obey God.* Like carrying a bag of rocks over my shoulder, the heaviness continued to weigh on my heart. Finally, I picked up the phone and called the first two companies and turned down both job offers. *Two down and only one more to go*, I thought. *Let's get this over with.*

I picked up the phone, one last time, to call the Dallas office. "Sorry, but I can't take the job in Dallas, I need to move back home to Tulsa after graduation," I said regrettably.

"Great!" The HR director responded. "We have a place for you in Tulsa," he continued. "We were trying to accommodate you, and our Dallas office was willing to take you in, but you'd be a better fit in our Oklahoma office."

After I picked myself up off the floor, I accepted the job. On my first day at work, when I stepped out of the elevator and walked into the reception area, I heard in my spirit, "Two years. You will be here two years."

God had a plan all along, but I had to stay on course. Unfortunately, if I had continued to follow my own way, I would have found myself out of place. God doesn't want any of us to get out of place.

The Right Fit

According to Ephesians 4:16, God perfectly fit us together. This means we are a custom fit for our role in the body of Christ. The problem comes when we get out of place and try to fit into a role for which we were not designed. This misalignment can have an adverse impact on our fulfilling

FINDING OUR PLACE

this Fourth Dimension of our Call—Understanding our Role. To highlight why it is so important to find the right fit and stay in our place, let's look at a story in 2 Samuel, chapters 15–18, about a man named Ahimaaz.

This story takes place during the reign of King David when his son Absalom tried to usurp the throne. He forced King David and his men to flee Jerusalem. Ahimaaz fled the city with him. He was the son of Zadok, the high priest who served David.

Later, Absalom gathered his army and pursued the king and his men. When King David was warned of the impending danger, he took refuge in a place called Mahanaim. Afterwards, the king dispatched Joab, his lead commander, and a battalion of men to confront Absalom and his troops in the woods of Ephraim. Ahimaaz went along with Joab and his soldiers. A fierce battle took place and ultimately Absalom was killed. When Joab was ready to inform King David that his son was dead, this dialogue between Joab and Ahimaaz took place:

> Then Ahimaaz the son of Zadok said, "Let me run now and take the news to the king, how the LORD has avenged him of his enemies." And Joab said to him, "You shall not take the news this day, for you shall take the news another day. But today you shall take no news, because the king's son is dead." Then Joab said to the Cushite, "Go, tell the king what you have seen." So the Cushite bowed himself to Joab and ran. And Ahimaaz the son of Zadok said again to Joab, "But whatever happens, please let me also run after the Cushite." And Joab said, "Why will you run, my son, since you have no news ready?" "But whatever happens," he said, "let me run." So he said to him, "Run." Then Ahimaaz ran by way of the plain, and outran the Cushite.
>
> —2 Samuel 18:19–23 NKJV

As the story continues, Ahimaaz gets to King David before the Cushite. The first question the king asked was if Absalom was safe. Ahimaaz answered, "I saw great confusion just as Joab was about to send the king's servant and me, your servant, but I don't know what it was."[1] Then the king told Ahimaaz to step aside and wait. Meanwhile, the Cushite messenger finally arrived. King David asked him the same question. The Cushite responded, "May the enemies of my lord the king and all who rise up to harm you be like that young man." Then the king retreated to his bedchamber and wept.

From this story, we are able to glean some principles that highlight the importance of understanding our role; to pursue the purpose for which we have been fitted and not a role that God did not intend.

I believe one of the reasons why Joab was so resistant to Ahimaaz delivering the news to David, was tied into Ahimaaz's calling, since he was a progeny of Aaron. God established Aaron and his descendants as priests for Israel according to Numbers 18:7, "But you and your sons, the priests, shall personally handle all the sacred service, including the altar and all that is within the veil, for the priesthood is your special gift of service."[2] Their duties included being officiators of worship, ministers at the altar, teachers of the law, and mediators for Israel.

Ahimaaz's calling meant that he had a distinct authority and anointing for priesthood—the purpose for which he was fitted. However, Ahimaaz moved out of place—out of his designated role—in order to operate in the role of a messenger; a purpose for which he was not fitted. This story teaches us seven principles to help us understand how important it is to pursue the right fit.

Calling Gives Insight

Principle #1 – When you are in the place for which you've been fitted, you receive vision for your calling. Dr. Myles Munroe defines vision in two ways. First, vision is, "the ability to see further than your physical eye can look." Second, "vision is what you keep seeing even when you close your eyes."[3]

The Cushite had vision. His role was a messenger, and God anointed him for this purpose. Joab told him to go tell King David what he saw. He saw what took place and understood what message to deliver. So he ran in his authority with purpose. He knew what had happened because he was in position to receive revelation and insight.

When we have vision, we see solutions when others see roadblocks. We see the diamond, when others see a lump of coal. We see possibilities, while others see limitations. When we're in our place, we see from a perspective others don't have.

Conversely, when we are out of place, our vision will be clouded. Ahimaaz had nothing to tell the king because he had no insight as a messenger. He told the king he was there but couldn't tell what had happened. This shows us, that when we're outside our place, we cannot see what God has not positioned us to see.

No Reward

Principal # 2 – There is no reward for being out of place. A good example was the NBA All-Star Game I watched on TV one evening. The superstar NBA players from the West were battling the superstars from the East. This event is different from the normal basketball season or even the playoffs. When the media interviewed one of the players at the end of the event, the player commented, "I'll be

7 DIMENSIONS TO FULFILLING YOUR CALL

glad when this is over with, so I can get back home for the playoffs."

I believe one of the reasons why this particular player felt this way, was because the All-Star event was only an exhibition game. It was like a scrimmage in which the outcome had no competitive value. This player's goal was the playoffs, in which he could compete for the NBA championship.

Joab questioned Ahimaaz's reason for delivering the message. He asked, "Why have you a desire to go, my son, seeing that you will get no reward for your news?"[4] There was nothing to gain. For Ahimaaz to take the message, was the equivalent of playing a scrimmage or exhibition game where the outcome didn't matter because there was no reward. We have to ask ourselves, "What things are we doing or pursuing for which there will be no kingdom value or reward?"

Taking Shortcuts

This leads to principle # 3 – Shortcuts are easy when one is out of place. I had been working about a year on the audit job, when I paid a coworker of mine a visit. It was his first year as well, however, I wasn't sure when or if I would see him again. He had started about a week before I did. We hit it off right away. Our friendship provided stability in my life during a very stressful time. I could tell he was a strong Christian and had a very keen sense of God's calling on his life. He always felt that being an auditor was only temporary for him, and that God was leading him to be a pastor.

"Hey RJ," I said as we greeted each other. As I stood in the doorway, I could see boxes everywhere. *Looks like he's packing for good*, I thought.

"Sorry you lost your job," I said sympathetically.

"Oh, don't be sorry; this layoff was God's plan," he responded, as he was wrapping some decorations. I was shocked that he was taking it so well.

"Now we know that God wants us back home in Florida to pastor," he continued. Wow, I thought.

"Well, as you know, I'm leaving to," I replied. This comment caused him to have a bewildered look on his face, but I was determined to convince him it was my time as well. I had been there thirteen months so far. The irony of it all was, even though the company executed three layoffs, I was still there and didn't understand why.

I tried to continue to explain myself. "This job is too stressful, and I'm tired of the hard work, late hours, and traveling eighty percent of the time, going from company to company, performing audits. I'm tired of the researching, reviewing other company's books, combing through pages and pages of paperwork, invoices, and documents, and ..." Before I could finish, RJ interrupted.

"But hasn't it only been a year?" he asked me. Right about this time I was standing, and he was sitting on his couch staring up at me.

"Yes."

"Didn't you say God told you that you would spend two years with this company?"

Wow, he remembered that conversation, I thought. I didn't know what to say. I shared with him in those first few weeks on the job about my experience of what the Lord said to me on my first day at work. RJ had a good memory.

"Yes, I remember, but things are different now," I stressed. "The work is overwhelming. God sees my suffering, and it's time for me to move on to better things."

Immediately, he stood up, grabbed my hand, and said, "Let's pray!"

I thought I should be praying for him; he's the one who lost his job. His prayer went something like this, "God, I ask for Your divine will in Kelvin's life. Don't let him miss Your opportunity. I pray that he obeys You."

I knew God had something for me on that job but, that was before reality set in—the challenging workload, long hours, and complete exhaustion. Despite what God said, after that first year, I wanted out. Unfortunately, I was trying to take a shortcut.

Ahimaaz took a shortcut. He was so determined to outrun the Cushite that he took an alternate route. He cut across the plains of Jordan to get to Mahanaim, where David was. Historians believe that because of the proximity of Mahanaim to the battlefield, it may have been easier to get to Mahanaim by way of the plains of Jordan, rather than running through the hills.[5] It was a much easier route than the path taken by the Cushite. In essence, he took a shortcut to accomplish what God had not called him to do. It represented his way of bypassing God's process in order to succeed in something that takes time to prepare for.

Also, this illustrates the danger of being outside our element. Being out of our own place, makes it easy to feel threatened by others who are in their places. We can have the tendency to become envious and competitive against those who are in their places. Our goal should not be to outdo one another, but rather, to compliment, aid, and build one another up.

Conversely, being in place creates confidence, boldness, and security in God. We must be careful to avoid impatience that can drive us in the wrong direction. The shortcut we take may turn out to be the longest route to our destination.

God's Way Is the Best Way

Similarly, when we are in the place for which we have been fitted, God turns the longest route into the shortest route which represents principle #4. The text implies that the Cushite took the longer and more rugged route as he took the mountain terrain to get to Mahanaim. It was the hardest way to travel to get to David. God's path for each of us may not always be easy. The process involves preparation, cultivation, and refinement, and He has a process set for each of us.

The auditing firm wasn't God's way of intentionally trying to make me suffer, but it was the long and rugged route He mapped out for my life, because of what He wanted to teach me. The glory God wanted out of my life was far more important than the temporary suffering I had to bear. He was trying to deposit something in me through that experience, that I needed for my calling. I had to make a choice to endure the set time and to stop trying to circumvent God's process.

Stop Fighting and Embrace God's Opportunity

Principle #5 – God's way is the best way. Let's expand on my earlier statement under principle # 1. God was not trying to give Ahimaaz a messenger's vision, but He was trying to give him vision for something else. You see, God did want Ahimaaz in Mahanaim. Ahimaaz was in the right place but in the wrong role and at the wrong time. It was the wrong time, because when he tried to deliver the message to King David, he was actually back in Mahanaim for the second time. God was not finished with him when he was in Mahanaim the first time, but unfortunately, he left too soon to follow Joab in pursuit of Absalom (2 Samuel 17:24).

Ahimaaz was a priest who was out of place and out of time. His father, Zadok, was the high priest in Jerusalem, so it was not Ahimaaz's time to serve in that capacity. God was preparing him, molding him into the high priest that he needed to be, and that preparation required patience. God was instilling vision for priesthood, but he wasn't finished with the refining process.

The reason why I believe Ahimaaz left Mahanaim prematurely is because when King David fled from Absalom, he left the Ark in Jerusalem under Zadok's care (see 2 Samuel 15:29). Now you have a king and part of his kingdom out in the wilderness. Wouldn't they also need the spiritual covering of a priest, just as they did in Jerusalem? I believe this was Ahimaaz's opportunity to serve as a priest for the king and his men in the wilderness. Though it was a harsh environment, the need was there. Remember, God chooses the training ground. Whether we like it or not, He knows what's best.

Unfortunately, Ahimaaz couldn't see the opportunity. He was too impatient to wait. He had his eyes set on another man's prize. Avoiding what God has for us won't make things less difficult, it's simply easier to embrace His plan. What may seem like a demotion, can turn out to be what God uses to promote us to our next level, if we're willing to endure the waiting period. Again, Ahimaaz was in the right place at first. However, when he left Mahanaim to go with Joab to battle, he displaced himself.

Wasting Time

Principal # 6 – Out of place means out of time.

In spite of what God told me, I wanted out of my situation. I submitted resume after resume to this company and that company. Instead of trying to get all I could out of where I was, I was trying to do all I could to get out of where I was. Despite all my efforts, nothing came about. Time was lost.

When Ahimaaz got to the king, he was told to step aside and wait. Despite all his efforts to outrun the Cushite, he still had to wait. Likewise, we may be busy, but if we're out of place, our efforts will be of little value in God's eyes.

Furthermore, Ahimaaz was on repeat. He left Mahanaim only to end up right back where he started, in Mahanaim. In our own situations, if we don't allow God to finish what He started in us, we may have to start over again or at least pick up where we left off, at a previous point in our life.

Principle # 7 – Ministry is made effective when it is fitted properly. When Ahimaaz delivered the message, it was a word that did not move the king, but when the Cushite delivered the message, it got the king's attention. The message moved the king to brokenness and changed the face of a nation. God wants to mature the gifts and callings in each of us, so we affect nations and our local communities.

To get where God wants us to be, takes total submission to His sovereignty. He knows what is best and what is the best route to get us there. We must endure the process to deliver a seasoned word, but this word must be weathered in us.

Found It

Somewhere along the journey, Ahimaaz allowed God to finish preparing him. Even though the Bible does not record much more about Ahimaaz after Mahanaim, we do see that he eventually found the place he was fitted for, as he went on to succeed his father in the priesthood.

> {Aaron's Descendants—} Only Aaron and his descendants served as priests ... The descendants of Aaron were Eleazar, Phinehas, Abishua, Bukki, Uzzi, Zerahiah, Meraioth, Amariah, Ahitub, Zadok, and Ahimaaz.
> —1 Chronicles 6:49–53 NLT

God is calling us to rise up and take our place in the body of Christ. God wants to stir up what's in us. He loves us too much to stop pursuing us. He's calling us to take our place. I understand that many times we don't agree with the process God allows us to go through. The path God has for us is usually so tight and narrow that it's tempting to venture off of it to seek something different, but we must stay the course.

You may even feel like you haven't found the right fit yet or that it's too late to fulfill your calling, but that's not true. All is not lost. No matter what mistakes we have made, it is never too late to make ourselves available for His service. We must continue to seek after God and search for Him with our whole heart, even if we're out of place. As with Ahimaaz, if we find ourselves out of place, God can ease us back in into position. God knows how to get us where He wants us.

I did end up staying with that auditing firm for the two full years. Exactly two years and one day later, I started working for a new company with better pay and better benefits. The bigger story was, I eventually realized why God wanted me to work for this firm back in my hometown, instead of the places I had originally chosen. He wanted me to serve in a ministry that He chose for me. I recognized that it was also my training ground. He was preparing me for my calling, for what I'm doing today.

Finally, a quote by William Gladstone says, "He is a wise man who wastes no time on pursuits for which he is not fitted."[6] I encourage you to pursue the purpose for which you've been fitted. God has a set place for you, so don't try to circumvent God's plan. Stay on course. You may find that what seems to be the longest route may actually turn out to be the shortest.

Chapter 8
7 Principles

1. You are a custom fit for your role in the body of Christ.

2. When you have vision, you see possibilities while others see limitations.

3. Be careful; don't let impatience drive you in the wrong direction. The shortcut you take, may turn out to be the longest route to your destination.

4. God's path for each of us may not always be easy. The process involves preparation, cultivation, and refinement, and He has a process set for each of us.

5. What may seem like a demotion can turn out to be what God uses to promote us to our next level to fulfilling our call, if we're willing to embrace it.

6. God wants to mature the gifts and callings in each of us so we can affect nations and our local communities.

7. No matter what mistakes you have made, it is never too late to make yourself available for His service.

THE FIFTH DIMENSION: TOTAL DEPENDENCE UPON GOD'S GRACE

CHAPTER 9

THE CALL DEFINES HOW WE ACCOMPLISH THE CALL

Having gifts (faculties, talents, qualities) that differ according to the grace given us, let us use them.
—Romans 12:6 AMP

THROUGH THE FRONT window of my house, I could see that John had arrived. As I stepped out the front door, he was stepping out of his car. I wondered if he would be in his normal, joking mood this early in the morning.

"What is it this time? Must be important to get me up on a Saturday morning," he said with a comical grin.

I knew John was just being himself, always kidding around to keep the atmosphere cheerful. He was my best friend and was more reliable than anyone I knew. As he continued walking up the driveway, what I called him for immediately caught his attention. He noticed my almost new British Sterling. It was nice and shiny but had a slight problem.

"Oh no," he hollered, pointing at the rear passenger side of my car. "You just bought it, and you already got your first flat!" He laughed, but then he thought for a moment.

"You called me for that?"

Unfortunately, it wasn't that simple. There was more to the story.

"No," I responded. "I don't need you to change a flat for me." I was trying to keep a serious face but couldn't help but join in the laughter. I guess I was laughing to keep from crying.

"I found the spare and the jack but nothing to take the lug nuts off with," I responded. Apparently, the jack handle was not included with my purchase. But I wasn't worried. John always had tools. His reputation was that there was nothing he couldn't fix.

Sure enough, John reached into his car and pulled out his jack handle, but this only led to another problem; it didn't fit. He returned to his car, pulled out a toolbox, and retrieved a 5/8 inch socket.

"Try this," he said.

I tried it. "Nope," I responded. Then we tried a smaller sized socket. It didn't fit either. We tried socket after socket but had no success.

Then John paused for a moment with a bewildered look on his face. He had a way of coming up with out-of-the-box ideas when he got that look on his face.

"Wait a minute! You've got to be kidding me!" He seemed excited. He ran to the car and pulled out another set of sockets, as if he was saving the best for last.

"Bingo!" he shouted. "Nineteen millimeters, a perfect fit. Metric. Who knew?" Then he handed me the ratchet with a final comment, "Now change your tire." Then he did what he always did; he sat, watched me work, and laughed.

I hadn't needed help changing my tire, but rather, I needed the right tool for the job. After many years, eventually, I sold that car, but to this day, over twenty years later, I still have that ratchet with the 19mm socket on the end.

It's a constant reminder of how important it is to have the right tool for the job.

In order to fulfill what we are called to be and to do, God equips us with the tools we need. These tools consist of God-given gifts, which are *endowed abilities that enable one to accomplish a task*. These gifts include our personality, natural talents, abilities, and passion. In addition, God equips us with spiritual gifts, and most importantly, with the Holy Spirit. Our gifts and talents empower us to be what we are and to do the work God called us to do. It's God's power unleashed.

Understanding you have these tools and the source of these tools represents the Fifth Dimension of The Call: Total dependence upon God's Grace. Let's talk about some of these tools.

What Motivates Us

Our personality is the first tool in our spiritual toolbox that God uses. Personality is defined as the totality of an individual's behavior and emotional characteristics. It's the complex characteristics that distinguish an individual.[1] God uses our personalities as a way to express what He has given us. Pastor Erik Rees asserts that God, "created all of us to relate differently, feel differently, react differently and to respond to life differently. He continues, "Your personality takes center stage in all areas of your life!"[2]

Secondly, God equipped us with natural talents or abilities. These are the things that we are good at instinctively. It's natural for us to be fluid with certain skills, because of the way we're mentally wired. Examples of natural skills include singing, dancing, speaking, cooking, painting, organizing, communicating, leading, facilitating, carpentry, and the list goes on. As you may have experienced, there are some things you do without effort and other skills you have to develop over time.

The third set of tools God puts in our toolbox are spiritual gifts. C. Peter Wagner defined spiritual gifts as an "attribute given by the Holy Spirit to every member of the body of Christ, according to God's grace, for use within the context of the Body."[3] Lists of spiritual gifts are found in Romans 12:6–8, 1 Corinthians 12:8–10, 28, Ephesians 4:7–13, and 1 Peter 4: 9–11. In his book entitled, *Spiritual Gifts*, author, Bryan Carraway explains that there are three basic purposes for spiritual gifts.

1. To serve one another in the body of Christ (1 Peter 4:10; Romans 12:13)
2. To enable each child of God to specialize in a certain ministry area for more effective service (1 Corinthians 12:7)
3. For equipping the saints (Ephesians 4:11)[4]

Spiritual gifts are contingent upon the work of the Holy Spirit in our lives. This means, we don't own these gifts; God owns them. As we yield to the Spirit of God, God uses us to bless others. Also, the differentiator between natural talent and spiritual gifts, is that natural talents can operate within a person without divine assistance.[5] Even people who don't know God have natural talents and abilities, but only the Holy Spirit can influence spiritual gifts.

Don and Katie Fortunes, authors of the book, *Discovering Your God-Given Gifts*, further expand on a unique set of spiritual gifts in Romans 12:6–8, categorized as motivational gifts. These gifts are listed as perceiver, server, teacher, exhorter, giver, administrator, and compassionate. The authors assert that these gifts are built into us and shape our personalities. They also say that each of us possesses at least one of these gifts.⁶ Further, these motivational gifts tune us into the myriad of problems in the world that need to be solved. These gifts are how we influence the world we live in to make it a better place.

For example, there are those who love to serve, like when Martha showed her love for Jesus by attending to His needs when He visited her house. Her goal was to cook, clean, and make Him feel as comfortable as possible. She loved hospitality. This was the gift of serving in action.

Others posses the teacher gift. This type of person is motivated toward learning and sharing knowledge with others. To a teacher, life is about helping others understand. That's what I enjoy doing.

Some additional tools in our toolbox include our passion and experiences. Collectively, all these tools make up what Rick Warren describes in *The Purpose Driven Life* as our S.H.A.P.E. (Spiritual gifts, Heart, Abilities, Personality, Experiences). The unique combination of these tools in our lives is the way God intends for each of us to serve Him.⁷ How well we blend these tools determine our effectiveness.

The Anointing

The last and most essential tool in our toolbox that makes all these tools work efficiently is God's anointing, which destroys every yoke (see Isaiah 10:27). Anointing figuratively means rich, thick grease, liquid, or oil. Oil is an Old Testament picture of the Holy Spirit. In other words, the anointing is the measure of God's Spirit in and on our life. Jesus had the anointing without measure (see John 3:34).

When God anoints us, He applies the oil for different reasons. In chapter 5, we noted the purpose of the anointing was to set an individual apart for God's use. In this chapter, we'll talk about a second application of the oil—to empower.

In other words, the anointing is an endowment of God's presence to complete a task. It's God adding His power to us so, we can succeed in fulfilling our call.

God Values His Oil

I rarely needed to change a flat tire on my British Sterling, but I did perform general maintenance on a routine basis, such as changing the oil. One time after changing the oil, I found oil leaking onto my driveway. As far as I was concerned, my car needed every drop of oil, so for me, this oil had value. I figured out that I had a leaking gasket. Of course with John's help, we fixed it.

God values the oil of His Spirit. There are a couple of things necessary for us to understand so that we can continuously experience God's empowering anointing.

First, to experience God's anointing, we must only do what we have been called to do. If we don't, then that would mean God is wasting His oil, but waste is contrary to His nature. In Genesis chapter 1, when God saw that the earth was without form and void, God put it back together so it could serve its purpose. Why? Because God doesn't waste His resources. When God anoints us, He has an objective. My point is that God never wastes His anointing. He will shut it off before He squanders it.

For example, in Second Kings chapter 4, there is a story about a woman whose husband died. She had lost everything, and because of her debts, the creditors were going to take her sons away as slaves. In her distress, she cried out to the prophet Elisha for help. He told her to find something in her house that could be used. She found a jar of oil. Then he instructed her to borrow as many empty vessels from her neighbors that she could get her hands on. Then in verse 4, he told her, "And when you have come in, you shall shut the door behind you and your sons; then pour it into all those vessels, and set aside the full ones."⁸

As she did what the prophet told her to do, she experienced a miracle. The oil kept flowing as she poured from one container to another. He told her that when one container was full, she should set it aside and fill another one so nothing would be wasted. The prophet represented the voice of God in her life, and as long as she did what she was supposed to do, the oil continued to stream out from her container.

But then something interesting happened when she ran out of empty vessels; the oil ceased (see verse 6). When there was nothing else to pour the oil into, there was no reason for the oil to keep flowing, so it stopped. This also implies that the oil didn't halt just because she ran out of empty vessels, but also because she stopped pouring. In other words, when she stopped doing what the prophet told her to do, the oil had to stop flowing, otherwise, it would have been wasted.

When we focus on our own agendas and stop doing what God has called us to do, then the anointing on our lives is not able to accomplish what it was sent to do. God will stop pouring rather than waste His anointing. What have you been called to do? As long as you're doing it, the oil will keep flowing.

You Are Unique to God's calling

Secondly, if we plan to continue to experience God's anointing, the key is in avoiding any attempt to emulate others.

There is a native Australian bird called a Lyrebird, which can imitate just about any kind of sound. It can sound like other creatures of the wild, but it can also mimic sounds like a "mill whistle, chainsaws, car engines and car alarms, fire alarms, rifle-shots, camera shutters" and the like.[9] If you were near one of these birds and didn't realize it and heard one of these sounds, it's possible you couldn't tell the difference between what was real and what was a copy.

Sometimes we can find ourselves like the Lyrebird, imitating others. In pursuing the call God gave us, it is imperative we do it the way God wants us to do it. We aren't to copy what someone else is doing, nor are we to strive to be something others want us to be. God called us because there is no one else like us.

God knew that Satan could not create. He could only imitate. This is why he made only one of us. Each of us brings uniqueness to the call God has for us. It's OK to be ourselves. It's OK if you can't preach, sing, teach, play, write, draw or simply do some things just like someone else can. But why should you want to be like others when there is no one else like you?

We can (and we must) learn from others, but we must be careful about how we emulate them. It's important to find out what God wants from us, because we can't flow in an anointing that has not been assigned to us.

In 1 Samuel 17, the story picks up where Israel is at war with the Philistines. The enemy had a champion warrior, Goliath. Everyone from Israel's camp, including their leader, King Saul, was not willing to fight Goliath because they were all afraid. Finally though, a shepherd boy named David, who wasn't afraid to confront this giant, stood up. When King Saul heard about David, he sent for him. Upon seeing David, the king questioned the lad's ability. King Saul perceived him as young and inexperienced, so he gave David his kingly armor to use. But David couldn't use it. The unfamiliarity of the heaviness and bulkiness caused David to pull it off. He confronted Goliath with his own bag of tools and defeated him (1 Samuel 17:39–40, 49–50).

Saul's armor symbolized his authority, capability, and anointing. Saul wanted David to emulate him. In essence, Saul was saying to David, "Do it the way I did it, that got me where I am today." When Saul put his armor (i.e. anointing) on David, he was trying to empower David to do something he had never even done, to go the distance in war he'd never been. But notice, if Saul had what it took to fight Goliath, then he would not have sent for David.

David told Saul he wasn't used to his armor. In essence, David's response to Saul was, "I cannot complete God's plan for my life in the way you think I should complete it. The end result of what God wants out of me may not be the same end result you want out of me but that's OK; I have my own defined end."

David recognized his own uniqueness. God gave him revelation of what he had in his own hands. He took up his own staff, bag, and slingshot (verse 40). God used what He had already been cultivating in David's life to accomplish what He called David to do. And because David accepted and agreed with the anointing on his life, he accomplished so much more. Saul had an anointing to slay thousands, however, David's anointing empowered him to slay tens of thousands (see 1 Samuel 18:7).

I had to accept and come into agreement with God about my callings. For example, in writing this book, there came a point in my life when I had to realize that I was so busy doing things for everybody else that this book God put on my heart wasn't getting done. I wasn't valuing the anointing in my own life. Proverbs 14:23 states, "There is profit in all hard work, but endless talk leads only to poverty."[10] God gave me a bag tools, and one of them was a pen. I had to use it and put into practice what God had been cultivating in my own life.

If David had followed Saul's way, he would have only operated in the anointing to slay a thousand and would have forfeited the tens-of-thousands fold anointing. Don't forfeit the anointing on your life. Don't limit God's call by trying to be like someone else. Remember, it's God's call, God's anointing, God's grace, and your uniqueness. It's OK to learn from the best, but then, become the best at what you do.

Grace Makes It All Come Together

I was determined to have a nice evening and anticipated having a great evening. My wife and I had visited this particular steak restaurant earlier this year, and we were looking forward to our date. The company was superb (my wife of course). The greeters were very cordial, but I should have detected an early warning sign. Once we were seated, I noticed food under and on our table.

Upon seeing our reaction to the slovenly kept area, our host said, "Oh, I'm sorry. Let me clean that." Afterward, we sat for a few minutes, then a few minutes more. Finally, our waitress came, greeting us with a nice smile.

"What would you like to drink?" she asked.

"I'll take iced tea, please," my wife responded.

"Water for me," I replied.

"I'll give you a few minutes to order," she said, and then, she swiftly disappeared. My wife and I chatted for a while, then the waitress finally returned to take our order.

My wife said, "I'll have the chicken salad."

"I'll take the steak, well done. Please make sure it's well done," I continued.

THE CALL DEFINES HOW
WE ACCOMPLISH THE CALL

Then I pulled out a coupon for 10% off my meal that I'd received in an email. I presented it to the waitress. She gave me a hint of a sneer. *Did I do something wrong?* I thought. *Maybe she's just having a rough day.*

She returned with a basket of only four rolls. Then the wait started once again. About a full thirty minutes passed before our salads were delivered.

"We'll take more rolls with our meal, please," I emphasized. Another thirty minutes passed before she delivered our food. Needless to say, I was very eager to get started.

My steak included mash potatoes and steamed spinach. It looked char-grilled. The aroma of this steak was calling my name. I grabbed my fork and knife, ready to feast. I cut into my steak, and I was shocked. It had a pinkish color in the center.

"But I said well done!" I responded exasperated.

We waited and waited until our waitress finally returned.

"Excuse me, but this steak is not cooked like I requested," I explained.

"Hmmm," she sighed. She grabbed my plate and took it back.

I called after her, "Oh, by the way, can you bring us more rolls?"

"Sure, we got some coming out of the oven now," she responded as she disappeared off into the sunset with my food. My wife was almost done eating her chicken salad when finally, not the waitress, but the manager returned with my re-cooked steak.

"We apologize for that, I'll make sure I you give a 10% discount off your meal," she remarked.

"Thank you."

Then our waitress walked by. I asked again, "Can we get some more rolls?"

"Got some coming right out the oven now," she responded again.

By this time, the evening was getting late, and we were ready to go. Our waitress finally materialized again. "Would you like some dessert?" she asked.

"No, can I have my check and a few to-go containers? Oh by the way, we never got our rolls," I firmly responded.

This time, along with our "to-go" containers, she returned with a basket of rolls—only four. *Wow,* I thought. *Only four rolls? Is she serious?* By this time, I felt unappreciated.

"Can we get some more rolls to go?" I asked.

"If I bring out more rolls, we will have to charge you for them," she responded with a serious look on her face. "We can only bring rolls out four at a time with your meal."

Then she handed me the check with no discount at all like the manager promised. I looked at my wife. Without saying a word, her eyes and her smile were telling me, "Calm down."

"I need to see the manager," I demanded. My well of patience had run dry. The waitress took our check and my coupon and swiftly walked off. A few minutes later, the manager returned with our check and a container full of rolls.

"We apologize for any inconvenience and please consider us again," she said.

By this time, we were ready to go as I handed her my credit card. Our waitress returned in less time, this time. My guess was that she was anxious for us to leave. She handed me the credit card receipt.

My mind was made up. I was determined to disclose my frustration with the service we had just experienced. I looked at the receipt but had to pause. Why did I feel a stirring on the inside? Despite all the noise in the restaurant, I could hear that the Holy Spirit was getting ready to speak.

Like a camera comes into focus, the empty space next to the tip line on the bill magnified right before me. Everything else was gray. I picked up the pen and felt led to write.

Why, I thought. *It's not fair. Her attitude wasn't right!*

Despite how I felt, at that moment, for some reason, I sensed that God wanted me to represent Him. Though undeserved, I had to push my feelings aside. I finally wrote in that blank space a twenty percent gratuity. Then I felt God's peace. God wanted me to display His love and for that waitress to experience a taste of what I've come to know as grace.

Grace Undeserved

Typically, we voluntarily give a waiter or waitress a monetary gift based on their performance, which means the gift is earned. But God gave the body of Christ gifts based on a different paradigm. In Ephesians 3:7, Paul said that God made him a minister according to the gift of grace. Gift is defined as divine gratuity. Additionally, grace is defined as favor or kindness shown without regard to the worth or merit of the one who receives it and in spite of what that same person deserves.[11]

Every one of us received a divine gratuity. God's grace removed from us the requirement to perform in order to obtain it. This means every spiritual gift and ability we have is based on His desire for us to have it, not because we earned it.

God's grace is not based on our significance, but rather on our insignificance. It's not based on our strengths but rather, our weakness; nor is not based on our wisdom but rather, our foolishness. It's God's ability in us to do what we can't do by ourselves. Grace makes heaven's resources available to us so that we are without excuse.

7 DIMENSIONS TO FULFILLING YOUR CALL

In First Corinthians 15:9–10, Paul explained, "For I am the least worthy of all the apostles, and I shouldn't even be called an apostle at all after the way I treated the church of God. But whatever I am now is all because God poured out such kindness and grace upon me."[12] Paul acknowledged God as the source of the gifts in his life. He recognized that who and what he was, was because of God's favor and love.

He also acknowledged that God was the reason for all of his accomplishments. In the later part of verse 10, Paul continued, "and not without results: for I have worked harder than all the other apostles, yet actually I wasn't doing it, but God working in me, to bless me."[13] The call on our lives necessitates our understanding that we are nothing without God. God is the source.

What Shall I Render?

David said it this way in Psalm 116:12, "What shall I render unto the LORD for all his benefits toward me?"[14] To render means to go back to the starting point. I believe David was acknowledging where he started, as a lowly shepherd boy, and comparing it to where he was in his final role, as king over Israel. In essence David was saying, "What can I render back to God for His favor, His love? What can I render back to God for protecting me from mine enemies, for believing in me when no one else did, and for keeping me when I didn't know what my future would be?"

How could David pay God back for all that God did? How can we pay God back for everything He's done for us? We can't! What He does for us is undeserved. We are able to do what we do because God favors us. God puts His Spirit on us to do great things, in spite of us. How He uses us for the kingdom doesn't compare to anything we give back to Him, but what we can do is give Him the glory.

The Key That Unlocks Grace

A few years ago, I took a team on a short-term missions trip to New York, to train in urban ministry with an organization call NYSUM (New York School of Urban Ministry). During that time, our group had the opportunity to work with inner-city kids, during a Vacation Bible School event. The lesson's theme for that day was about Joshua and the battle of Jericho. The class instructor asked me if I would take over and teach the six to eight year old kids, the lesson for the day.

Who me? I thought to myself. *I'm not good with kids. My wife is incredible with kids; ask her.*

Reluctantly, I started talking to the kids about Joshua, and immediately, I could tell they were bored. I felt they were probably thinking, *Who is this guy? Can somebody make him stop?*

It was at that point, all I could do was pray, "Oh God, show me a creative way to reach these kids." Almost immediately, God gave me an idea.

"OK kids, stand up," I said. They shot up out of their chairs, probably thinking it was over and time to go outside.

"Now, take your chairs and put them in a circle," I said.

It was then, the bewildered looks began to show on each child's face. I wasn't sure where I was going with it either. "Now march in one big circle around the chairs, and as you march, make the loudest sounds possible." Now the children's leaders in the room were really confused.

"And when I say stop, everybody knock the chairs over!"

I could tell some joy just entered into the room. A glow began to radiate from their faces, especially from those of the boys. So around the chairs we went, marching and making as much loud noise as we possibly could.

Suddenly I cried out, "Stop!"

Then without being prompted, the kids scrambled in chaos. They were screaming, kicking, and pushing chairs over. Crash! Bang! It was as if somebody dropped fifty cymbals from the ceiling. Then there was a pause.

"That's what God did to Jericho's walls when the children of Israel blew the trumpets!" I shouted. "The walls came crashing down!" I had their attention now. From then on, I was able to finish the lesson.

The key to why I'm telling this story is what happened at the end of each day. All the classes gathered together in the main sanctuary for a grand finale and the children were asked to volunteer to share what they had learned in class. Two of the kids from my class stood up and ran to the microphone to tell everybody what they learned. I sat in the back of the sanctuary with the biggest grin on my face thinking, *Maybe I'll hear something about our demonstration with the falling chairs*. On the contrary, I didn't hear one comment about that; nothing. My grin turned to disappointment.

That evening as I wrote in my journal, the Holy Spirit brought that moment back to my mind and asked me a question, "What was I expecting those kids to say?" I paused and thought. I realized that I was expecting a pat on the back of some sort for the good job I felt I had done. It was then, the Lord opened my eyes to recognize that deep down in my heart, I wanted some kind of credit for what the kids learned and experienced that day. My expectation came from pride.

Pride, the Enemy of Grace

I had to acknowledge my pride and repent for not giving God all the glory due Him. We have to be alert and resist the subtle temptation of self-importance. James 4:6 tells us that "God opposes the proud, but gives grace to the humble."[15] The quickest way to shut off the fountain of grace is to walk in pride.

Pride is toxic and puts our will at the center of focus. It causes us to think, perceive, and act in ways that can become destructive to our relationships, our ministries, our future, and ourselves. It's pollution to our calling.

God tells us we can defeat pride by submitting to Him and resisting the enemy. Humility is the key to the strength we need to overcome self-importance. Andrew Murray said that humility is "the place of entire dependence on God, is … the first duty and the highest virtue of man … without this, there is no true abiding in God's presence or experience of His favor and the power of His Spirit."[16]

Humility is essential to experiencing more of God's grace. God gives grace and more grace to those who are low enough to receive it. But to stay in the right place to receive this grace requires diligence on our part. Andrew Murray continues, "Humility is not a thing that will come on its own. It must be made the object of special desire, prayer, faith and practice."[17] It starts with our attitude. Our constant acknowledgment of our need for God is the key to understanding this Fifth Dimension of The Call, which will keep us in total dependence on grace.

Chapter 9

7 Principles

1. Our gifts and talents empower us to be what we are and to do the work God called us to do. It's God's power unleashed.

2. The anointing is an endowment of His presence to complete a task. That task is your calling.

3. It's OK that you can't preach, sing, teach, play, write, draw, or simply do some things just like someone else can. But why should you want to be like others when there is no one else like you?

4. Your accomplishments may be similar in comparison to others, but they're not the same by God's definition.

5. Grace makes heaven's resources available to us, so that we are without excuse.

6. God puts His Spirit on us to do great things, in spite of us. The call on our lives necessitates our understanding of that point—we are nothing without God.

7. Our constant acknowledgment of our need for God is the key to understanding this Fifth Dimension of The Call, which will keep us in total dependence on grace.

CHAPTER 10

STEWARDS OF OUR GIFTS

I PULLED MY dad's car into the driveway after returning from yet another trip of driving around the city with my friends. Ever since I had gotten my driver's license, I felt like I had to use it as often as possible. I was behind schedule for when I had to return the car. Dad wanted to make sure Mom had a ride to work.

As I entered the front door, I could see directly into the kitchen. Dad was asleep in his favorite place, right in front of the hot stove, after a long, hard day of work at a construction site. It was winter. He sat there getting warm with his feet propped up.

I tried to tip toe through the living room, so when he woke up, he would think I had been there the whole time. Of course, he woke up before I could sneak past him. He looked over at me, and I could tell by the way his jaw jutted out that he was ready to say something. I'd seen that look before.

"Son, did you put gas in the car?"

"Ah, no Sir."

"When you borrow someone's car, you should always put gas in it." Dad began to fix his chair and repositioned himself in a more comfortable position. "Don't just drive someone's car. Instead, give it back to him in a better condition than when you borrowed it."

"Was I supposed to wash it?"

He looked at me and smiled as if to say, "What do you think?" He then turned back toward the stove, and within seconds, he fell back to sleep.

I learned the value of stewardship that day.

What my dad was trying to help me understand was that it's important to be a good steward. Learn to take care of something that belongs to someone else while it was in my custody. That's being a good steward.

Jesus told a parable in Matthew 25:14–30, which exemplifies the importance of good stewardship from another perspective. The story is about a wealthy master who was about to embark on a long journey. Before he left, he entrusted talents to three of his servants. To one servant, he gave five talents, to another, he gave two talents, and to the third servant, he gave one. Then he left them with the responsibility to improve on the talents he gave them.

While the master was away, the first two servants invested their talents and doubled what they had. The servant with five talents increased his to ten. Likewise, the servant with two increased to his four. But the last servant with one talent was afraid to do anything because he didn't want to risk losing what the master had given him. Instead of investing the talent, he just buried it in the ground.

When the master returned, he wanted to find out how they had managed what he had left them. He praised the first two servants for multiplying what he given them. He considered them faithful and rewarded them. The servant who had done nothing was rebuked. The master considered him to be unfaithful, made him give up what he had, and punished him.

Lessons Learned

This parable of the talents is a metaphor of how we as Christians are to maximize our God-given gifts. In fact, Christian stewardship entails the responsibility of investing whatever time, talents, and possessions God has given us to yield the best returns for Him.[1]

Christ, the Master, left us with talents in the form of gifts. Again, our gifts include spiritual gifts, natural talents and abilities, and personality traits. We've also been gifted with passion, skills, experiences, and more. From this parable, observing what the servants learned and understood, we can glean some principles that will aid us in maximizing our God-given gifts toward fulfilling our call.

Value Your Gifts

Point number # 1 – The servants had to understand the value of what they been given. A talent was a weighted coin. Ten talents were worth about twenty years' worth of wages.[2] So, it had extreme value. God has invested gifts in each of us and we need to see His investment as valuable. For instance, your personality is God's gift to you and is important to your call. Your experiences add value to your calling. Even the negative ones are important, as God can turn your lemons into lemonade, creating testimonies in your life that can refresh others. We must value each of our gifts.

Accountable for Your Gifts

Point number #2 – The servants had to recognize where the talents came from in order to be accountable.

The servants didn't find these coins on a beach or under a rock. They didn't create them; neither did they inherit them. Their master left them these talents. Each servant was accountable to the master.

Likewise, we are answerable to God for the gifts He gives us. We may feel these gifts are ours, and we own them; we decide what to do with them. But I have news: God is the source of all that we have both tangible and intangible, and He wants us to yield our gifts to Him.

As previously mentioned, our gifts are a direct result of God's grace (see Romans 12:6). That's why in this Fifth Dimension of The Call of Total Dependence Upon God's Grace, we're reminded that it's only by the grace of God that we have capabilities. We are accountable to God for the potential inside of us.

Recognize Your Gifts

Point number #3 – The servants had to appreciate what they had been given in order to increase it. The problem with the servant who received one talent was that he didn't understand nor did he appreciate what he had. He couldn't fathom any profit potential because he misjudged what one talent could accomplish. I imagine he thought, "One? Why one? What is one coin going to do for me? I can't see any benefit in using this." He couldn't discern the potential of what he had.

Unfortunately, sometimes we don't realize what we have. God doesn't want us to make the same mistake as the one wicked servant. As good stewards, He wants us to understand the potential we hold. In other words, we must recognize the gifts God has given us.

God wants the discovery of our gifts to become a reality. For example, authors, Marcus Buckingham and Donald

Clifton, talk about how important it is that we realize our natural talents and turn them into strengths. They emphasize that "the real tragedy of life is not that each of us doesn't have enough strengths, it's that we fail to use the ones we have."[3] Researcher, George Barna, affirms, "Imagine what might happen if nearly half of all believers had a clear and firm conviction that God has given them a supernatural ability to serve Him in a specific manner. If more believers understood the nature and potential of that special empowerment, the global impact of the Christian body would be multiplied substantially."[4] Dr. Myles Munroe sums it up perfectly by saying, "No matter how big the world is, there's a place for you in it when you discover and manifest your gift."[5]

Ways to Discover Your Gifts

A few of the ways we can discover our gifts are by:

1. Surveys and Questionnaires
2. Serving Others
3. External Influences
4. Inward Satisfaction

Let's elaborate on each one. First, surveys and questionnaires are tools uniquely designed to aid us in identifying our gifts. I found some helpful books with simple exercises, which gave me insight into my own gifts and how and why I think the way I do. These resources were beneficial in clarifying what I knew in my heart, as well as, discovering answers to questions I have always had. These suggested resources are found in Appendix 1. This information will help you identify the following:

- Spiritual Gifts
- Natural Talents/Strengths
- Personality Traits/Motivational Gifts
- Passion/Desire/Interest
- Core Values

Keep in mind, these resources can't tell us everything about the potential we hold, but we can definitely take steps, and in some cases, leaps, in the right direction toward understanding our gifts, so we can move forward toward fulfilling our calling.

Secondly, serving is a means by which we can discover where we best fit and what we're good at. Pastor Rick Warren affirms, "Many books get the discovery process backwards. They say, 'discover your spiritual gift and then you'll know what ministry you're suppose to have.' It actually works the exact opposite way. Just start serving; experimenting with different ministries, and then you'll discover your gifts. Until you're actually involved in serving, you're not going to know what you're good at."[6] So we ought to look around in our church or community, find a need, and meet it; see a vacancy and fill it. As we look for ways to help someone else, we'll find ourselves converging with our gifts.

Thirdly, God can use external influences like other people to help us discover our gifts. That influence may be a parent, family member, teacher, coach, pastor, or friend. In my early teenage years, some of my favorite times were spent enjoying guest singers and music groups who ministered at our church. I remember one Sunday evening as if it were yesterday. My interest was riveted, and I couldn't help but stand at attention as I watched this particular drummer play with amazing sophistication and style. He ended the song they were rehearsing with a drumroll and crash of the cymbals, with such rhythm and timing, it was like I listening to the percussion section of a live marching band. He had a captive audience—me. I didn't realize that this particular evening would turn out different from every other evening I had spent at church.

The drummer stepped off the drums and approached me. I didn't know what to think? Was he going to autograph his drumsticks and hand them over to me? Or was he going to pour oil on my head like the prophet Samuel did to David, and within an instant, I would have his talent? Perhaps not, but I could tell he had something to say. Maybe he would be like king Solomon and share such a nugget of wisdom that I could use it and would one day put me in the drummer's hall of fame.

"What's your name?" he asked.

"Who me?" Of course, I was the only one standing in front of the drums and had probably been his biggest distraction.

"I want you to play a song during worship this evening," he said.

I paused. That's it? That's the nugget of wisdom? No oil? No autograph? However, as Jesus did to Peter, he was telling me to step out of my boat. "But I can't play drums," I responded.

"Try." It was that simple. His one word was a gentle yet direct command: try.

Of course it was easier for him than for me, but I did try. That evening when it was my time to play, I slipped behind the drum set and proceeded to play. I imagine the folks in the audience probably asked, "What happened to the drummer?" because even though I was on the drum set, there were two obvious problems. First, although the drum set was directly on the stage, all you could see was the set. I don't know how you can play and hide behind a drum set to avoid being seen, but I'd found a way. Sitting on the drum seat, I was bending down as far as my agile teenage body would allow. I was so scared that I refused to be seen. The second obvious problem was that I couldn't be heard. Why? Because, I didn't want to be heard. I tried to play as softly as I could. As far as I was concerned, I needed to play as if I was in the same room with my infant baby sister asleep in the crib. I had better not wake her up.

Believe it or not, that night was the beginning of my life as a drummer. I often think about how God used that great, drumming brother to recognize my music potential and to encourage me to get out of the boat and try. I had been trying to bury my gift because of fear. God can and will often use others to help us discern our potential. He sends opportunities our way to get us to recognize and accept our gifts.

What Is in You That God Is Calling For?

Finally, a sense of satisfaction in what you're doing is fundamental to discerning what your gifts are. The movie, *Chariots of Fire*, based on a true-life story, was about two men who represented Britain in the 1924 Olympic Games. These men were incredible athletes and had won gold medals in track and field. The difference between the two men was their motivation. The first character, Harold Abraham, was running to prove himself. He felt like the world was against him. He ran for himself. However, the second character, Eric Liddell, ran to honor God. He made a statement that he believed God made him for a purpose, and God made him fast. He said, "When I run, I feel His pleasure."

What is it in you that when you're doing it, you feel Gods pleasure?

Ecclesiastes 3:11 tells us that God set eternity in our hearts. In other words, He planted the seed of purpose in our hearts, so that satisfaction will only come from cultivating that seed. In, *The Principles and Power of Vision*, Dr. Munroe explains that "there is something in you that is being called by eternity."[7] Something in us cries out to be fulfilled. This piece of eternity drives the passion, the desire, and the dreams that occur over and over in our mind, even when we're awake. These are indicators to uncovering what we're gifted at doing.

Investing Yourself

This leads point # 4 – The two servants invested in themselves first. Just a few years out of college, a coworker of mine said to me, "Hey, you should invest in this company. They specialize in frozen yogurt."

"Frozen yogurt? I never heard of such a thing." The rise of the interest in frozen yogurt wouldn't have been something I kept up, especially since I'm not a big fan of yogurt.

"Yep, you can double your money!" he emphasized. Then he continued to rant and rave about how much money he made in just a short period of time.

"Double my money!" I responded. That was all I heard. I took my savings, rent money, car payment, bill money, and all I could scrape up, and called a broker. I set up an account and invested all my cash into this company that made this unique product—frozen yogurt.

The prospect was too good to be true ... and it was. Little did I know that this co-worker had a family member who was a part of the senior management in the company. Also, my coworker neglected to tell me that the stock had already peaked and was declining. In a short time, the stock stabilized at a much lower cost than what I had invested.

"Hey, what happened?" I asked some months later. "What happened to the great investment that was supposed to double my money?"

"Oh, just be patient. Wait it out. The market will turn."

"Patient!? How long will that take?"

"Possibly a few years," he responded in a serious tone.

I couldn't wait a few more years. I needed to eat! I called my broker and sold my stocks. Needless to say, I lost money. I got back around sixty cents for every dollar I invested minus brokerage fees. It was evident that I was inexperienced at investing. Back then, I could have used a book like, *Investing for Dummies,* to reduce my level of obliviousness.

I don't believe the two servants blindly and unwittingly invested in just anything. Because they understood what they had in their hands, they didn't leave it up to chance like I did. They needed to know what they were doing to have a fighting chance at profiting or at least at minimizing any losses. They had to know where to invest and where to trade. After all, it was their master's money they were managing. I believe they devoted themselves to learning and researching. They did their homework. They invested in themselves.

When the master confronted the servant who did nothing with the talent left to him, he told that servant he could have at least deposited the money in the bank to earn interest. In other words, that was the minimum that could have been done. This implies that the other two servants went beyond doing the minimum and did the maximum that could be done to earn the most profit. They took on more risk for greater gain.

The first two servants must have researched the markets and formulated a strategy. Did they invest it all in one place or did they diversify? The nation of Israel was the hub of a thriving economy. It's believed that Israel's "geographic location made the nation a strategic corridor through which all military and economic traffic between Europe, Asia, and Africa had to pass ... it was impossible to ship anything anywhere between Asia Minor, the Mesopotamian Valley, and Egypt without going through Israelite-controlled territory."[8] It was the Wall Street of its day.

The servants were in the right place to make money, but they had many choices. Where would they choose to trade? Would they deal with the agricultural industry of Israel or the livestock commerce of Palestine? Maybe they invested in the transportation market, such as, camels and donkeys, as they were the U-Haul choices of that day. How about the food industry? Olives, grapes, figs, and raisins were popular commodities during this time. Or would they invest in businesses that catered to the major trade routes, in order to profit in the import and export arena? The salt mining industry was an option because of the Jordan Valley and the Dead Sea. How about the timbers of Lebanon? What about investing in the shipping industry in the Mediterranean Sea or in Galilee's fishing business? My point is, the servants had to decide which markets to trade in, in order to yield the best outcome. These servants had to have done their homework.

The Master's Goods

I don't believe the master left it up to chance, but in every way, made it possible for his servants to succeed as they cared for his money. He invested in the servants so they could invest in themselves.

First, he distributed talents according to their capabilities. This suggests the servants earned his trust. Think about what this means: this master was wealthy for a reason, and

I'm sure he didn't just give his money away at random. Can you imagine the tabloid headlines back then printing, "Rich Man Entrusts Three Slaves with His Wealth." On the contrary, he had to have understood what the servants were capable of, but how? Perhaps he had invested time in them. Possibly, the servant's abilities were pulled out of them by way of the master's observation, training, and mentoring. He recognized the potential in each and distributed in proportion to what they were capable of doing.

Secondly, the master left the servants his goods (see Matthew 25:14). Goods represented his estate and his property. It's also defined as, "gifts and endowments, whether original or acquired, natural or spiritual."[9] In other words, the servants had access to everything the master had. It was as if the master were saying, "I left you my goods and gave you abilities to take these talents and maximize them for the benefit of my kingdom. Now go turn your talent into something more."

I believe the goods were his way of empowering them to accomplish what they would need to accomplish. These goods included tangible resources, like his estate. These servants, perhaps, had access to his library, his trade journals, company annual reports, 10K filings with the Jerusalem SEC, audit statements, the master's contacts, his financial advisors, etc. You may be saying, "Ok Kelvin, aren't you exaggerating a bit?" The point is, I don't believe the master left it up to chance but left the servants plenty of resources, and it was up to them to take advantage of those resources. In other words, the talents were needed to turn a profit, and the goods were everything they would need to be successful. God has invested gifts into us, and He expects us to invest ourselves in our gifts. We invest in ourselves by developing our gifts.

Develop Your Gifts

It's our responsibility to cultivate our gifts. The unfaithful servant returned the talent the same way he got it—undeveloped. In order for our gifts to be used to their fullest potential, we have to invest in ourselves, and that requires our time, our energy, and our effort.

The reason why we can invest in ourselves is because God invested in us. First, God (our Master) endowed us with our gifts. Secondly, God left us His goods. This means He left us everything we need to be successful—naturally and spiritually—has been made available to us by God. One theologian said, "To give eminent gifts to persons incapable of properly improving them would be only to lead one into a snare."[10] God didn't give you gifts just to make you frustrated, but rather, He invested in you, and He expects a return on His investment.

God made available intangible resources. Do you need wisdom? It's available. According to James 1:5, "If any of you lack wisdom, let him ask of God, that giveth to all men liberally."[11] Do you need favor? It's available. According to Second Corinthians 9:8, "And God is able to make all grace (every favor and earthly blessing) come to you in abundance."[12] How about just an opportunity? According to Matthew 7:7, "Ask and it will be given to you; seek and you will find; knock and the door will be opened to you."[13] God will make opportunities available.

Next, God made tangible resources available to meet our every need, and those resources are in the earth already. Dr. Myles Munroe said, "God never requires from you what He does not already have in reserve for you ... God may have provisions all over the world waiting for you."[14] God held nothing back. We have all the resources available to develop and succeed with our gifts.

7 DIMENSIONS TO FULFILLING YOUR CALL

Since everything we need is already in the earth, what do we need to develop our gifts? God has people waiting in the wings because they're called to help you. You see, before the famine of Egypt could exist, Joseph had to be in his place, which means, for every problem, God already has a solution on the earth.

In order for there to be a teacher, there must be a student. For example, ever since I was in high school, I've had the desire to play bass guitar. I had opportunities, off and on, to use this musical talent, but I never really developed it. When I finally made the decision in my heart to pursue this gift, I stumbled on the business card of a skilled bass player in the area, whom I had met several years earlier. When I called him, he was more than willing and able to take me on as a student to help me nurture this gift.

When we're ready to be a student of our gift, God will raise up a resource, such as, a teacher, coach, mentor, or parent to pull out of us, what we need to enlarge our gifts. The seed of potential is already in us. God will put someone in our lives to make a difference, so we can make a difference.

I believe when we're ready to take our gifts to the next level, God will make other resources open up, such as, the right opportunities, jobs, ministries, or volunteer possibilities. Because the master already left it for us, this means it's all around us, but we have to work for it. In other words, we may have to drive a few miles to get it. We may have to go to the library to read it. We may have to enroll in class to learn it. We may pay an instructor to understand it. We may need a coach to captivate it. We might have to invest to acquire it. But rest assured, whatever we need is already available. I didn't say it was close, or that it was free, but it's there. God has resources in place for us.

Utilize Our Gifts

Point # 5 – The first two servants invested all they had. They took their coins to the marketplace and labored in trading. They used their talents to their fullest extent to reap the maximum possible benefit. This tells us that we have to use our gifts. We must employ them to reap the maximum benefit for the kingdom. When we engage in our gifts, we benefit in three ways.

1. The kingdom of God benefits as God gets the glory. Matthew 5:16 states, "Let your light shine before men, so that they may see your good works and give glory to your Father in heaven."[15] This means using our gifts is a form of worship to God. Romans 12:1 tells us, "I exhort you, therefore, brothers, in view of God's mercies, to offer yourselves as a sacrifice, living and set apart for God. This will please him; it is the logical Temple worship for you."[16] When we use our gifts, we are in essence saying, "God, I'm giving you my best—myself. I am taking what You gave me and am giving it back to You. Be glorified in what I do."
2. Others benefit when we use our God-given gifts. In order for others to benefit, we have to establish this chief principle: A gift is never about the person who possesses the gift. When gifts and talents are all about the person, we're glorying in them for selfish gain, and then who gets the glory from it? Erik Rees, author of the book *S.H.A.P.E.*, says, "If your actions benefit others, you are serving with love. If you realize you are the prime beneficiary of your actions, you need to immediately realign yourself with God."[17]

God gave Joseph the ability to interpret dreams, but the gift wasn't about Joseph. Joseph could have sat and interpreted his own dreams all day long, but where would that have gotten him? Nowhere! But as Joseph understood that his gift was to benefit others, he yielded his gift to God. Furthermore, God's use of Joseph was about what He wanted to accomplish for the people of Israel not what He would accomplish just for Joseph. So now, who was the real interpreter of dreams, Joseph or God? It was God. Joseph was merely a vessel yielded to God to accomplish God's work.
3. We benefit. Because Joseph used his gift when he helped the butler and the baker, his gift got him an audience with Pharaoh, and he was ultimately made second in charge of Egypt. So in the end, Joseph benefited also. When we use our gifts for the glory of God and to benefit others, we get something out of it as well.

Taking Our Portion in the Earth

> Every man also to whom God hath given riches and wealth, and hath given him power to eat thereof, and to take his portion, and to rejoice in his labour; this is the gift of God.
>
> (Ecclesiastes 5:19 KJV)

Our gifts represent authority and empowerment. For a man to take his portion in the earth is a gift. God created this earth with an abundance of resources to supply humanity and meet every need. Just like the Promised Land God gave to the children of Israel, God gave us capabilities in the form of gifts and talents to possess the land that he has promised each of us. Our gifts give us the opportunity to take our portion of wealth in the earth.

Regarding the wicked servant who did not earn anything from his master's talent, the master told him that he was expecting to reap where he had not sown seed, and gather where he had not strawed. This point relates to each of us in terms of God establishing His kingdom in areas of the world that are still not under the authority of Christ. There are still people who have not heard the Gospel of Jesus Christ.

God wants the body of Christ to dominate all arenas of life, such as, music, art, and sports—things that have influence over people. God also wants his people to influence the areas of science, medicine, politics and much more. Our gifts enable us to take possession of what God hasn't taken charge of any arena where Satan has greater influence over people. For example, our schools have not been the same since prayer was removed. Our communities that are overturned by crime and poverty are areas the devil targets, but God wants us to take these areas back. The master reaping where he had not sown, also paints a picture of land that has not been tilled or cultivated. For us, this means there are new grounds and new dimensions yet to be discovered.

God promised to give the children of Israel the Promised Land, but it was occupied by the heathen nations. He gave Israel power and might to possess the land. What was interesting was that they could only possess it a little at a time, so that the land would not spoil or waste. God is saying that your gifts will enable you to possess what He promised, but a little at a time. In other words, when you're faithful with the least, more will be added.

How to Define Success

Jesus said in a similar parable in Luke 19:13, that we are to "occupy till He comes." This means we are to do business with the resources entrusted to us.[18] It's not about what we don't have to work with; it's about what we do have. God gets pleasure when we use what we have. Words to an old song written by Andre Crouch say that "little becomes much when you place it in the masters' hand." Luke 16:10 affirms, "Unless you are faithful in small matters, you won't be faithful in large ones."[19]

Let's get back again to the wicked servant who couldn't see profit potential. Another problem was that he had a narrow perspective of profit and success. In the same way, God wouldn't have given us gifts if He didn't think we could improve upon them, but we have to understand how God defines profit and success.

Not everyone is gifted to be an NFL star or an Olympic gold medalist, or to earn the Nobel Peace Prize, even though our gift could and most likely earn us money. But everybody's gift will turn a profit for the kingdom. We define profit in terms of monetary gain. However, there is no money in heaven. God defines profit as a soul, which means all of Heaven celebrates when it turns a profit, i.e., when a soul comes into the kingdom (see Luke 15:6–7).

Furthermore, we have a tendency to define success by how much we amass. Unfortunately, we are inclined to measure success based on volume, such as, the number of people, books, CDs, likes, how many hits to our website, how big our audience is, sales, ratings, income, viewers, etc. These counts are relative to our personal benefits and statistics. Indeed, we have to be good stewards and be accountable for the resources with which we've been blessed. If all those numbers are our main focus, we can lose sight of what God considers the important measure. Remember, both of the first two servants increased in different amounts related to what their master had given them, yet both were admired for being faithful. This tells us that our true measure of success in God's eyes is not based on volume, but rather, on faithfulness.

In, *The Purpose Driven Church*, Rick Warren defines success as, "bearing as much fruit as possible given your gifts, opportunities and potential."[20] God measures the quality of our work (the heart, motive, attitude, and obedience). Whether our gift enables us to reach the masses or to reach the one, what matters is our faithfulness to His calling and not how many products we sold. In Matthew 7:17–23, Jesus says that "many will say to me in that day, 'Lord, Lord, have we not prophesied in thy name? And in thy name have cast out devils? And in thy name done many wonderful works?'" In other words, there will be those who tell God to look at their track record, statistics, data, and numbers. Again, it's not about the numbers as much as it is about being obedient to produce the kind of fruit God is looking for from us.

Remember, abilities are what God puts in us to be successful, while the goods are what He makes available for us to be successful. We are to be faithful and accountable for what we've been given, so we can hear our Master say one day, "'Well done, my good and faithful servant. You have been faithful in handling this small amount, so now I will give you many more responsibilities. Let's celebrate together!"[21]

Chapter 10

7 Principles

1. Our gifts are a direct result of God's grace.

2. Often, God can and will use others to help us discern our potential. He sends opportunities our way to get us to recognize and accept our gifts.

3. God invested gifts into us, and He expects us to invest ourselves into our gifts. We invest by developing them.

4. When we're ready to be a student of our gift, God will raise up a teacher, a coach, a mentor, or a father, so that person can pull out of us what we need to be successful.

5. Our gifts give us the opportunity to take our portion of wealth in the earth.

6. Whether our gift enables us to reach the masses or to reach the one, what matters is our obedience to His calling, not how many products we have sold.

7. Remember, abilities are what God put in us to be successful, while the goods are what He makes available for us to be successful.

THE SIXTH DIMENSION: FOLLOWING GOD'S SOVEREIGN WILL

CHAPTER 11

THE CALL DEFINES WHAT WE ARE TO ACCOMPLISH

> For we are God's workmanship, created in Christ Jesus to do good works, which God prepared in advance for us to do.
> —Ephesians 2:10 NIV

"WHAT DO YOU want to be when you grow up?"
"A lawyer," she said.
"What do you want to be when you grow up?"
"I wanna be a doctor," he responded.
"What about you? What do you want to be when you grow up?"
"A policeman!" he shouted.
"A teacher," she said.
"Great!" I responded. "Go pick out your book bag!"
Whenever I worked with young people in our youth program, it was a special moment for me to hear their answers before they walked over to the table to pick out their free backpacks filled with school supplies. I always asked for their first name, what school they attended, and

what they wanted to be when they grew up. One little girl even said that she wanted to be a ballerina.

God used us that day. The program was always held on the last weekend before school started, and thank God that the particular weekend I'm speaking of, turned out to be a sunny day. I didn't know what we would have done if I had had to cancel this event, because there had been a series of thunderstorms all week long, including the night before. I was concerned the grounds would be too saturated to put up the tents and the inflatable for the kids to play on. I was concerned that no one would show up, but God worked it out. The ground was dry. The park and recreation crew had even cut the grass.

The excited volunteers showed up. They didn't let the threat of bad weather stop them from sowing their labor of love. Some helped unload the truck, set up the stage, and arrange the tables and chairs. I couldn't have asked for a better group of folks with which to work. The generator for the snow cone and popcorn machines was ready before I knew it, and we had plenty of soft drinks, snacks, supplies, and much more. The greatest miracle was that the community and all the kids met us in the park that day for our annual "Back to School Bash."

Giving out school supplies to at-risk kids was just a sample of some of the things we did. It was our way of rolling up our sleeves and putting our hands to work for the kingdom of God. It was an idea that God gave us to sow tangible seeds and the gospel into the lives of these children in this particular community. It was our opportunity. We were doing good works.

Following God's Sovereign Will (this Sixth Dimension of the Call) determines what we are supposed to achieve. But to realize it, we have to engage in good works.

THE CALL DEFINES WHAT WE ARE TO ACCOMPLISH

Called to Work

> And let our people also learn to maintain good works, to meet urgent needs, that they may not be unfruitful.
> —Titus 3:14 NKJV

In his letter to Titus, Paul emphasized the importance of maintaining good works for continued fruitfulness. This note of encouragement still speaks volumes to us today. Good works means valuable or worthy labor. To maintain means to practice. Just like the fundamentals of a sport or the elementary theories of music, practice enables one to apply what one has learned until the craft is perfected. And practice requires consistency. So for the kingdom, we should consistently engage in worthy labor. God expects to be able to work out of us, the active salvation He has worked in us, in the form of good works.

But who determines if our labor is worthy? God does. Ephesians 2:10 states that we are God's handiwork re-created in Christ for good works. In other words, we were designed, equipped, and appointed to not only do good works, but rather, our God-given assignments. Those alone determine the significance of our labor from God's viewpoint.

Performing activities outside of God's purpose and direction adds no value to the kingdom. In, *Ordering Your Private World*, author Gordon MacDonald talks about how some make the mistake of equating doing things with being successful. Activity and success are not the same. In actuality, some of us are "fueled by drivenness and not by calledness."[1] MacDonald expressed his own struggle to keep the right perspective and the right balance. He states:

> "That drivenness has created a moment of crisis for me down through the years. And each time I had to come to grips with fresh new revelations of an insidious energy

within me that wanted to achieve and accomplish things for reasons that were far from obedience to Jesus or the glory of God ... I had to learn how to listen to God and assure that I was moving according to His agenda and not my self-serving one."[2]

Like Pastor MacDonald, we need to evaluate ourselves because we can sing in the choir, be on the usher board, or even support various charities in a financial way but still feel empty. In spite of numerous activities, we can still lack peace, joy, and fulfillment and even feel drained. Though you're doing things for God, if your activities are out of alignment with what God has called you to do, satisfaction can never be achieved. Why? Because there is still something God has called you to do that has not been completed. The good news is that to make sure we're working on the right assignment, God does the following:

1. **He gives us the desire** – God will put what He wants us to do in our heart. He gives us a drive for what He wants. (Philippians 2:13)
2. **He reveals His plan** – God will confirm what activities He wants us to be involved in to keep us on the right track. (Ephesians 5:17)
3. **He gives us His Holy Spirit to lead us** – God promised to lead us into all truth. He gave us a helper, His Holy Spirit, who will guide us, teach us, and empower us. (Roman 8:14)
4. **He prepares us for the tasks** – As we are actively pursuing God's plan, He is always preparing us through various life experiences and leading us down paths of preparation. (Proverbs 24:27)
5. **He gives us the opportunity to achieve the tasks to which He has called us** – God will always

open a door for us to do what He wants us to do. (Ecclesiastes 3:1; John 9:4)

The Right Work Energizes

Working on the right assignment will energize us. Our passion is ignited because God is involved. This excitement creates a powerful motivation and unquenchable drive that's insatiable because it's divine. We can sense God's excitement when we are working on the right thing.

Paul talks about this heavenly fuel in the book of Colossians. He labored in preaching, teaching, writing, and establishing churches. His work was intense and responsibilities were vast. He labored until he hit exhaustion, and yet in spite of all the difficulty, there was something in him that pushed him forward. He was powered by something beyond any natural origin; God's energy was his internal power source.

> This is my work, and I can do it only because Christ's mighty energy is at work within me.
> —Colossians 1:29 TLB

Paul was striving, but he wasn't striving as if he was treading water to stay afloat. Like an Olympic swimmer in a 400mm race, he pressed forward to win the prize. That energy invigorated his passion and intensified his desire to see God work through him. We are motivated by that same energy source.

Philippians 2:13 reminds us that we tap into that divine energy when we are pursuing "His good pleasure." God's pleasure compels us. Author, Laura Beth Jones, said, "When we are called to do something beyond the thought of our own survival, special energy comes to our aid."[3] When we're working on the right assignment, we connect to a source of peace, inspiration, and energy that pushes us through the obstacles, the struggles, and the difficulty that we may encounter along the way.

The Right Work Creates Joy

Secondly, working on God's assignment produces what the writer of First Peter describes as an "inexpressible joy that comes from heaven itself."[4] When Tim Tebow was quarterback for the Denver Broncos during the 2011 season, he was interviewed after a win. The commentator complimented him on his success as a young, starting quarterback who, at that point, led his team in winning four out of five games. The commentator asked him how he was able to keep it all in perspective. Tim's response was:

> "We're very excited about the wins ... we're very passionate as you can see me playing out there today, I love it and I care about it ... but I think the greatest thing with this sport and with the NFL is we have such a platform, we can take that platform ... we can influence the next generation. And that is honestly my passion and you know this week we got to announce ... I was building a hospital in the Philippines; and this game means a lot but that hospital means more to me because that's changing people's lives ... giving people faith and hope and love ... that's more important."[5]

You could feel the excitement in Tim's interview; the joy he radiated as he talked about how God was using him to complete part of the good work he's called to do, to serve as a role model to young people and to serve those in need in the Philippines. His gift was enabling him to accomplish the work and is making a difference in people's lives. The thrill of a roller coaster ride can't replace, nor can money compare to, the joy we'll experience when we are working on God's assignment for our life.

The Right Work Affirms Our Purpose

Finally, working on the right assignment affirms our purpose.

Pastor MacDonald also talked about the time he put his hands to work assisting the Salvation Army relief workers with the recovery efforts at Ground Zero after the 9/11 catastrophe. He described the chaos all around them and how firefighters worked endlessly, 24/7, pouring through rubble in search of people who may still have been trapped alive. He described the focus, diligence, and passion of relief workers, and how they refused to give up hope. He and his wife were apart of it. It was at that moment he sensed purpose being fulfilled in what he was doing. He pulled his wife to the side and stated, "I was made for this!"[6]

Author, Laura Beth Jones, expressed this same idea as "when you are surrounded by that state of grace where nothing else matters except that feeling you have within yourself that is your intersection with destiny."[7] There is no better way to satisfy purpose than to work on the things you know God created you for; knowing that you were born for this. Those moments are worth fighting for and worth making time for. Destiny is worth pursuing.

What Structure Are We Building?

There is a mansion located in California called the Winchester Mystery House. It was built for the late Mrs. Winchester whose family owned the company that made the Winchester Rifle. This home has some unique peculiarities, such as bathrooms without plumbing and windows inside the house. Other irregular effects include "stairs that lead to the ceiling, doors that go nowhere and that open onto walls, and chimneys that stop just short of the roof." Some rooms were continuously remodeled. "It is estimated that 500–600 rooms were built, but because so many were redone, only 160 remain." It's also noted that the home never had an inspection and was built without any blueprints.[8] Oddly, this mansion was under construction for thirty-eight years.[9] It's noted there were no architectural designs. Basically, you could say this home was built without the end in mind of what it would finally look like.

In 1 Corinthians 3:10–15, Paul warns the Corinthian church of the importance of keeping the end in mind when it comes to building in God's kingdom. In this letter to the church of Corinth, Paul considered himself a skillful builder as he laid the foundation of Christ—the foundation for our faith. Furthermore, Paul warns the church to be careful about how they build on that foundation. He compared their teachings to building a structure and warned them to be careful of the type of structure they built.

Paul continued to emphasize that on the Day of Judgment, God will test every man's work (the spiritual structure built) by fire to determine the material used. So if the church of Corinth's teachings were aligned with the truth, it was like building a house using material such as gold, silver, or precious stones. These unique substances can handle fire. In fact, fire can improve their quality. Whereas, if their teachings strayed from the truth of what Paul had established, it was like building a structure out of materials such as wood, hay, or stubble, and unfortunately, fire would consume a structure made from these. In fact, these types of materials are normally used to stoke a fire. The end result would be no reward.

This same building analogy Paul used, we can use to describe the work God has called us to complete. We are workers together with Christ. As we work on our God-given assignments, we are in essence building something together with God, and He holds us accountable to do our part.

Our spiritual structure is the ministry that God has called us to do. This structure may be people, a mission, a business, an outreach, a church, a family, etc. Whatever ministry God personalized for us to do, on that final day, we will have to give an account. The people who praise us or criticize us today will not be the ones judging us on that day. God has reserved that right, because He alone gave out the assignments.

The Moffat translation of First Corinthians 3:14 says, "If the structure raised by any man survives, it will be rewarded."[10] As builders, if we expect to receive our rewards, we have to consider what our house looks like from God's perspective? Are we building ministry based on what God had in mind or are we building without a plan? Like the Winchester mansion, is our spiritual house built with bathrooms without plumbing, stairwells that lead to nowhere, or windows inside the house? The spiritual house we build will have to pass God's inspection.

Building Inspection

Where we used to live, one of my neighbors built a beautiful add-on to the back of his house. This project took him several months to complete. He spent late night hours after work putting his heart and money into the effort. He spent his weekends and multiple vacation days working on it until he finally got his new addition finished. He was proud. He did it without using any contractors. Some months later after pulling into my driveway upon returning home from work, I saw him outside working in the yard.

"Howdy neighbor!" I shouted. Immediately he made a beeline toward me.

"They're impossible!" he shouted.

"What's up?" I asked.

"The homeowners association and the county! They're impossible to deal with." OK, I thought. I've never seen him so irritated.

"They refuse to hear my side."

What are we talking about? I thought.

"They told me I had forty-five days to comply, or I have to tear it down. Do you know how much money I spent? How much time? And they want me to fix it or else!"

I was speechless. The building inspector disapproved his new addition. Because he didn't follow the homeowners' association rules and county codes, the add-on was considered non-compliant. My neighbor had two choices: put more money into correcting the problems or tear it down all together.

The "fire test" that Paul refers to in 1 Corinthians 3:13 is like the process required of us by a building inspector. Most states require that all builders follow certain building codes for new construction and additions to ensure their structures are safe and durable. Further, the permit must be obtained before you can even build. A permit is an authorizing document, by the state's jurisdictions, granting someone permission to build. Finally, after building, a state or county authorized inspector is usually required to inspect the new structure to ensure it meets certain building codes. Only then will the new structure be certified for occupancy.

The inspector (the fire) is going to determine if our works (the spiritual structure we raise) meet God's specifications outlined in His divine building codes.

Inspectors examine everything: the quality of the foundation, the structure itself, and the materials used. First,

Jesus Christ is the only spiritual foundation on which we can build our lives and ministry; there is no other spiritual foundation. Second, God will inspect the materials used to build our spiritual house. If our house was fabricated as a result of pride, it may not survive God's inspection. If jealousy is the material used to build our spiritual house, it may not pass inspection. If our spiritual structure was built out of disobedience, it may not pass inspection. We may put in a lot of time and effort, but like my neighbor experienced, what started wrong, despite all the time, money, and effort, may well end wrong.

As previously stated, before we can start building legally, we have to get a permit that will grant the permission to build. So before we build our "spiritual" structures for the kingdom of God, we need to ensure that we have our heavenly permit. This permit is God's authorization—His perfect will.

Finally, after we build our structure, it's due for an inspection. God's inspection will determine if what is built is in accordance with heaven's building codes. This inspection is required, as it will determine who gets the glory—God or someone else. If God is pleased, then there's a reward waiting.

God Builds the House

> Unless the LORD builds the house, they labor in vain who build it; unless the LORD guards the city, the watchman stays awake in vain.
> —Psalm 127:1 NKJV

This verse in Psalm 127 tells us that if God doesn't build the house, then our labor is in vain. In other words, if God is not involved in what we're building, then we are wasting time. Secondly, the Psalmist emphasizes that it's God who builds the house. But if the Lord builds the house, then why is our labor even necessary? Because the house that God is building is in heaven. He needs us to build it on earth. You see, what God builds in heaven is the design for what our spiritual structure on earth is supposed to look like. He calls each of us to execute the plan on earth according to this heavenly pattern.

Build According to Pattern

I'd just gotten home from middle school when I walked in the door and once again, I could hear the machine grinding. It was a unique sound of thread intertwining between fabrics, but it always depended on the fabric's thickness and whether the pitch was high or low.

What was she working on this time, a suit, dress, curtains or blanket? Is it for a new customer or a regular? I thought. I knew what was coming next, so I'd try to make a mad dash to my bedroom, hoping she didn't notice me.

"Hi son. How was your day?" she'd asked.

"It was okay," I would respond.

"Good. As soon as you drop off those books, change your clothes and run to the store for me."

"Ah Mom, can I eat something first this time?"

Sure enough, just as quickly as I said it, she'd put a sample piece of fabric in my hand.

"Get me twelve yards of this. And I need a pattern. Get me pattern number ..." She'd rattle off some number.

I was not sure how she always knew what she wanted or needed. We didn't have the convenience of the computer or the Internet back then, but she always knew. Sure enough, I'd run to the store, give the clerk the cut-out fabric from my mom, and say it just like my mom said it, "I need twelve yards of this please. Then, I need pattern number ..."

It only took a few moments before the store clerk would hand me back my request. Then I'd take a look.

Oh, it's a dress this time, I thought. Most times, I was right.

I could always tell how mom's sewing venture would turn out; I'd just look at the picture on the front of the pattern's package. On to the cash register I'd go.

As soon as I got home, I'd hand mom the store bag. Like clockwork, she'd unroll the new material onto the cutting board. Then she'd remove the pattern from the package, lay it across the material, reach for her straight pins right out of that tomato-shaped pincushion, and start pinning the pattern to the material. Finally, to let the whole household know it was time for her to go to work, she'd start singing one of those old church hymns, "Precious Lord, take my hand, lead me on." Then she'd start cutting the material according to the dimensions of the pattern.

Before I could get away, she'd say with the biggest grin on her face, "Give me my change!" By the time I'd walked back to my bedroom, I'd hear that grinding sound again; her sewing machine was whirring in full gear. Hours later, or sometimes days later, I'd see Mom's finished product hanging up in the kitchen doorway. Every project Mom did turned out just like the picture I saw on the package, because Mom always made her masterpieces according to the pattern she had been given.

Everything Begins with a Pattern

Everything begins with a pattern. Walt Disney envisioned a theme park before he actually built it. It was said that "Disney drew sketches of his ideas for an amusement park where he envisioned his employees spending time with their children."[11] He asserted, "I just want it to look like nothing else in the world."[12] Walt Disney's dream came to pass, and it had all started from pictures he had envisioned in his mind. These mental images were transformed into sketches representing the pattern or model of what Disneyland looks like today, and it is like nothing in this world.

All patterns have a source. They start as God-given visions, dreams, or ideas. When God wants something done on the earth, He will plant a picture in the heart and mind of a person. That picture becomes the pattern to follow. Keep in mind, a spiritual pattern is more than what something is supposed to look like. It also reflects the essence and purpose of what God had on His mind. As a result, His pattern becomes our guide to fulfill the call of what God wants us to achieve on the earth.

Dr. Oral Roberts is another testament of a man who had great vision and who followed God's pattern for building. He built a university. He heard God instruct him, "Build Me a university. Build it on My authority, and on the Holy Spirit."[13]

I believe these instructions were more than just a to-do list; they were heaven's pattern that outlined the purpose for the university. One day Dr. Roberts transcribed on a piece of paper what God had in mind, "Raise up your students to hear My voice, to go where My light is seen dim, and My voice is heard small, and My healing power is not known."[14] Since its inception in 1965, Oral Roberts University's (ORU's) graduates have been impacting the world for the kingdom of God all because one man followed the heavenly pattern that he had been given.

The Heavenly Pattern

> They serve at a sanctuary that is a copy and shadow of what is in heaven. This is why Moses was warned when he was about to build the tabernacle: "See to it that you make everything according to the pattern shown you on the mountain."
>
> —Hebrews 8:5 NIV

THE CALL DEFINES WHAT WE ARE TO ACCOMPLISH

Moses followed heaven's pattern for building the tabernacle. God gave him explicit instructions from which he could not deviate. Why? Because God wanted the tabernacle on earth to be an exact replica of what was in heaven. While Moses communed with God on the mountain during a 40-day fast, God planted a picture in his heart—a glimpse of the heavenly sanctuary; a model of what the earthly tabernacle was supposed to look like.

God gave Moses the design, the blueprint, the building codes, and the permit, and Moses followed it to the letter. Exodus chapters 26–30 cover some of the specifics. Moses had to construct the tabernacle out of certain types of wood and, in some cases, over lay it with gold. Everything had to be a certain length, width, height, and depth (see Exodus 26:2). God required that the curtains, the veil, and all the fabric coverings be made out of specific materials and certain colors. Also, God was very specific about the furniture pieces that were used, like the Ark, table, golden candlestick, and altar. Moses had to be exact, as the tabernacle and all that was in it was a shadow of heavenly things.

In fact, this tabernacle and all the functions of the priesthood that God later showed Moses actually represented something greater. It symbolized what would take place in time and more importantly, what had already taken place by design. It was the model of redemption that was planned out before the foundations of the world. And like Moses, we have to follow the heavenly pattern God gives us.

In Luke 11:2, Jesus encouraged the disciples to pray for the heavenly pattern "as in heaven, so in earth."[15] As it is in heaven means according to the design God established. In essence, Jesus was telling us to pray for the building codes, so we can build on earth according to heaven's specifications.

Time to Build

When God gives you a vision, dream, or concept for something, that's His way of passing the baton. It's His way of putting the work into your hands for you to do. God will give you an idea of how to build your spiritual structure, i.e., a ministry, a people, a marriage, a family, a school or a business. However, He requires that you follow the design you've been given, so when you build it, it looks just like the model in heaven.

Dr. Oral Roberts once said, "When God is ready to do a new work in the earth, He causes a baby to be born."[16] This means your birth is evidence that God had something in mind for you to do. And like Dr. Roberts and many others, God wants you to leave a legacy. He intends for the work He's called you to do to outlast you and to affect your world—for today and for future generations. So enjoy executing the works God prepared in advance for you to do.

Finally, in his book, *Maximize the Moment,* Bishop Jakes emphasizes the importance of following God's pattern. He asserts, "The ultimate success is accomplished when we get to the end of all building and struggling of life and find that the house we built looks like the design we have been given."[17]

Chapter 11
7 Principles

1. God is working active salvation into us. He wants to work that active salvation out of us in the form of good works.

2. Though we're doing things for God, if those things are out of alignment with what God has called us to do, satisfaction can never be acquired. Why? Because there is still something God has called us to that has not been completed.

3. When we're working on the right assignment, we connect to a source of peace, a source of inspiration, and a source of energy that pushes us through the obstacles, the struggles, and the difficulties that we may encounter along the way.

4. Neither the thrill of a roller coaster ride nor money can replace or compare to the joy we'll experience when we are working on God's assignment for our life.

5. Before we build our spiritual structures for the kingdom of God, we need to ensure we have our heavenly permit. This permit is God's authorization—His perfect will.

6. Keep in mind, a pattern is more than what something is supposed to look like. It reflects the essence and purpose of what God had on His mind. As result, the pattern becomes our guide to fulfill the call of what God wants us to achieve in the earth.

7. When God gives us a vision, dream, or concept for something, that's His way of passing the baton. It's His way of putting the work into our hands for us to carry out.

Chapter 12

GOD NAVIGATES OUR COURSE

I will instruct you and show you the way to go; with My eye on you, I will give you counsel.
—Psalm 32:8 HCSB

IN, *ALICE IN Wonderland*, written by Lewis Carroll, there is a conversation between Alice and a Cheshire cat. Alice is at a fork in the road, and she asks him, "Which road do I take?"

"Where do you want to go?" he says.

"I don't know."

"Then it doesn't matter. If you don't know where you are going, any road will get you there."[1]

Have you ever felt like you were not quite sure where you were going in life? How about the times when you knew the destination, but you weren't quite sure how to get there? To know where you're going, you have to know the will of God for your life.

The good news is that God has set our destination and has given each of us the ability to stay on course. Following

God's Sovereign Will represents the Sixth Dimension to fulfilling The Call.

Earlier in chapter 5, I spoke briefly about how Jesus pursued God's will. God wants us to do the same, however, there are times when some aspects of His will are obvious, while at other times, we find ourselves questioning like Alice in Wonderland. When we feel this way, James 1:5 reminds us, "If you want to know what God wants you to do, ask him, and he will gladly tell you, for he is always ready to give a bountiful supply of wisdom to all who ask him; he will not resent it."[2]

When we're unsure, it's OK to ask God questions like, "Which way do I go? Am I on the right track? What's next for my life?" If we're willing to ask, God is ready to show us. But be prepared, because we may only get a glimpse, a nugget, or a thought of what's next. Oftentimes, God will share in phases because He wants us to walk by faith, one step at a time.

In order to take these steps of faith, God gave us three indispensible, navigational tools to keep us on course. These tools enable us to lock into God's divine will. He will guide us down the path toward fulfilling our call. Let's explore the first directional tool.

Road Trip

"My wardrobe is intact. Luggage packed? Check. Suits in garment bag? Check. Undergarments? Check. Toiletries? Check. Shoes and socks? Check. Not a cloud in the sky. A perfect day for road travel. Oil change. Check."

This will be the longest trip my family and I have ever been on, I thought. We're traveling from the Atlantic to the Grand Canyon, from the east to the west, from Virginia all the way to Arizona.

I checked to make sure I had my laptop, books to read, and the ice chest was full with lots of my favorite, highly caffeinated drinks. The time finally came, the van was packed and loaded, the family climbed in, and we were ready to go. The final check focused on my wallet, my glasses, and the map. Where was my map?

We were about to take the longest road trip of our lives, and in some way, I managed to misplace everything the AAA travel agency gave me—the map, the trip kits, and tour books. Even though I knew the destination, these things were essential because I had no clue of how to get where we were going. Without those tools, especially that map, I was unwilling to take the risk, especially across the country.

So we searched and searched and eventually found it; of course, it was packed away in one of the countless luggage bags we had stuffed in our minivan.

God never intended for any of us to venture out in life without guidance. Otherwise, we'd risk making wrong turns and making wrong decisions, resulting in costly delays, or even worse, missing our destination altogether. So the first navigational tool God left us, to help navigate our course toward fulfilling our call, is a map—His Word. Psalm 119:105 says, "Your word is a lamp for my feet and a light for my path."[3] God's map serves us in three ways:

1. God's Word is a Guide – God's word is like a flashlight that lights the path ahead so we can avoid stumbling. God reveals Himself through His Word. When we're in the dark, not knowing what to do, confused about which way to go, or finding obstacles hindering us, we can have a testimony like the Psalmist who cried out to God, "Direct my footsteps according to your word."[4] God's Word will light our way.

2. God's Word Provides Counsel – While heading to Arizona, I used the map to advise me on the correct interstate, turns, and exits. It helped me make the most appropriate decisions at the most fitting times. God Word provides counsel, and His counsel stands forever. It provides the wisdom we need. God promised if you mediate on His Word day and night "then you will be prosperous and successful."[5]
3. God's Word is a Locator – While on the road to Arizona, at any point, I could determine where I was, based on the city I was near and the interstate I was on, in relationship to the map. God's Word will illuminate our understanding of our surroundings and of where we are in life, as each pertains to our calling.

Distinct Paths

> In all your ways acknowledge Him, and He shall direct your paths.
> —Proverbs 3:6 NKJV

Because there were multiple routes to Arizona, I reached out to AAA, the travel professionals, to map out the best route—a distinct route to get me there in a timely manner. The consultants outlined routes on the map around major highway construction areas and identified the most scenic routes that would make the long journey joyful. Likewise, there are many paths to take in life, but God promised to make it clear as to which path to take at various points in our lives. He promised to show us the path that will lead to life, but we have a part to do to gain this understanding. Our part is to acknowledge and to consider (see Psalm 16:11; Proverbs 3:6, 4:26).

We acknowledge God by including Him in our decision-making. We lean on Him by going to the map of His Word. Feeding on His Word can guard us against making impulsive choices, as we patiently wait for His answer.

Our other part is to consider where we are. Proverbs 4:26 says to "carefully consider the path of your feet and all your ways will be established."[6] The writer was encouraging us, that in order to know what the next step is, we have to ponder where we are, the current path we're on, and where it's leading us. God gives us the opportunity to correct our course, but we must be willing to acknowledge how we got to where we are in the first place. When change is required, but we're unwilling to make that change, alter our behavior, or revise our decision-making, we might find ourselves back in the same predicament, days, months, or even years down the road. When we acknowledge the travel professional of life, God our Creator, who knows what's best for us, we make room for Him to direct our steps and to keep us on that well-defined route.

A Compass

Yosemite National Park is one of nature's greatest wonders. It consists of over 747,956 acres and is famous for its waterfalls, streams, meadows, mountains, and plant life, and is home to over 400 species of animal life. It's especially popular for its 800+ miles of hiking trails, and attracts hundreds of visitors and hikers every year.[7]

This park even has its own emergency response team called, The Yosemite Search and Rescue Team, which comes to the aid of those visitors who need help from time to time. In fact, over sixty percent of the rescue missions involve rescuing hikers who have been injured and/or have gotten lost.[8] In some cases, the hikers are lost due to not having a map, but in other cases, they didn't have another essential tool for hiking, a compass. One professional outdoor expert said, "With knowledge of a map and compass skills, hikers can keep themselves on track and avoid becoming a rescue statistic."[9]

The second tool God left us, to help navigate our course toward fulfilling our call, is a spiritual compass—His peace. God gave us His peace to help us circumvent any risk of getting lost in life or veering off our designated path. A basic compass has a magnetically-sensitized needle in the center that points north, based on the earth's magnetic system. The will of God is the strong magnetic pull, always pulling us toward God's purpose and design. God's peace is like that magnetic needle within the compass, pointing us towards His will so we can stay on course.

God's Peace

When I was in college, during the summer months, I interned with the Pepsi Company. Toward the end of my internship, I was sent to company headquarters in New York to meet up with other interns to learn more about the company. One evening we were treated to dinner and a cruise around New York. It was my first experience being on water. We weren't on a ferryboat; we were on a yacht. Down in the bottom of this luxury craft was a dining hall, where we were treated to dinner and music. There was a dance floor, but of course the food had my attention—steak and lobster.

The whole experience was exciting because here I was, a college kid, being treated as first class. The food was good, the music was nice, but what really blew me away was when several of us made our way out from the cabin onto the deck of the yacht. Once I stepped outside, there was a moment I'd never experienced before. Hearing the boat power through the water, everything was calm, still, and peaceful. It was like a holy hush came over everyone. Like me, all the students were mesmerized by the stillness of that peaceful moment. All we heard was the water separating as the bow of the yacht made its path. Birds were singing as they flew over us, and the wind sent a gentle breeze. Nature was making its indelible impression on our minds, sending us a message as if to say, "Relax, be still, nothing matters but this moment." Inside me, there was an incredible calmness and an inner tranquility.

That's what it feels like when we're in the center of God's will. We experience peace, which is a state of tranquility or quiet.[10] Being in the center of God's will produces a calmness on the inside despite what's happening on the outside. God gives us peace as proof we're in His will.

Like an Umpire

We can find security in God's peace. In game two of the 2010 World Series, the Texas Rangers were playing the San Francisco Giants. In one particular instance, one of the players for the Giants was at bat. The Ranger pitcher threw his pitch at what seemed like lightning speed. Then the next thing you heard was a "crack," as the ball and bat converged together. A grounder headed toward second base. The Ranger's second baseman lunged forward, took a spin on the ground, and pulled up the ball into his glove. He jumped to his feet, and instantly, while the batter dashed toward first base, he threw the ball to the Ranger's first baseman.

Simultaneously, as the runner tagged the base, the first baseman lunged forward to catch the ball. It looked like the runner made it first, but then, it also looked like the first baseman caught the ball first. The timing was impeccable. Was the runner for the Giants safe or was he out? From all angles, it was hard to tell. The first base umpire made the call. "Out." That settled the issue because the umpire made the final decision.

According to MLB regulations, the umpire has the authority to regulate a baseball game and to enforce all the rules of a game, including the World Series. Neither the fans, players, nor the coaches can overturn an umpire's decision.[11]

Colossians 3:15 states, "And let the peace of God rule in your hearts, to which also you were called in one body; and be thankful."[12]

To rule means to act as an umpire. God's peace is the umpire that rules our hearts. Secondly, "Heart" figuratively means "the soul," which encompasses our thoughts and feelings and our will and conscience, and that's exactly where we need peace.

God's peace will umpire your thoughts and decisions. His peace makes the final decision.

Additionally, the umpire arbitrates between the two opposing teams. Just as an empire keeps harmony in a baseball game, God's peace keeps harmony in our hearts by taking two opposing wills—our will and God's will—and joining them together.

The enemy will always try to make you feel that you've struck out or that you'll never make it to home plate, but rest assured when you are in God's Will, the peace of God is the final authority to let you know you are safe.

Trust God

Staying in the center of God's will requires trust. Proverbs 3:5 tells us to "trust in the LORD with all your heart, and lean not on your own understanding." Trusting

God means you're willing to put your confidence in Him. Would you give a total stranger your wallet or purse? Probably not. Why? Because you don't trust that person. However, would you give your spouse or best friend your wallet or purse? Why? We trust them. We have so much confidence in that spouse or best friend that we're willing to entrust to them what's most dear to us.

To trust God means to entrust your future, your life, and your calling into His hands and to believe He will keep His word to you. To trust God means that you have the utmost confidence in Him, that even if you were blindfolded, He could lead you by the hand through uncharted territory.

In the book, *The Power of the Call*, Henry Blackaby talked about his experience as a pastor and a mission's director, and his journey in following God into the unknown through various assignments and challenges. He explained the way he viewed it saying, "Our call was to Him (God), not to an assignment ... God's way was always the best way, the right way ..."[13] Trust will help us endure the unknowns.

Crystal Lewis encapsulates it in a song she wrote called "Trust Me" from her album, *Fearless*. The chorus says:

> Trust me, though you can't see,
> You can trust me, the way may be steep
> You can trust me, let me lead. Trust me.[14]

Trusting God will pervade any fear or doubt, because God promised never to leave or forsake us. Isaiah 12:2 tells us, "Behold, God is my salvation; I will trust, and not be afraid: for the LORD JEHOVAH is my strength and my song; he also is become my salvation."[15] So we can take our map and compass, go after our call, and trust God no matter what. And just in case we still get lost on the way to where we're going, we have no cause to worry; God has us covered. He left us a third navigational tool to get us back on track.

Instructions in Real Time

> And your ears will hear a word behind you, "This is the way, walk in it," whenever you turn to the right or to the left.
> —Isaiah 30:21 NAS

Traveling on business with a coworker of mine, I was driving the rental car, trying to find a particular manufacturing plant, using directions I had printed from the Internet. Consequently, what should have been only a twenty-minute drive from the airport turned into a monumental feat. I knew my destination, but I didn't know how to get there. About an hour and a half later, my coworker suggested that we pull up to a convenience store and go the old-fashioned route—ask for directions.

Upon entering the store, I observed two clerks behind the register, busy helping a long line of people. *So, I won't ask them*, I thought.

Meanwhile, other customers were pacing back and forth in the store, so I didn't want to disturb them either. Then my attention was drawn to a guy standing in front of the cappuccino machine. He was dressed in a brown uniform with a logo displayed on the front of his shirt pocket and his sleeves indicating he was a city worker.

Great, he should know his way around this place, I thought. So I approached him.

"Sir, how do I get to this manufacturing plant?" I asked.

He looked at me, thought for a moment, then responded, "Yeah, I know where that is." Then very confidently he proceeded, "You go down this road, make a right, go up on the bridge, then veer to the right a couple of feet, then make a left. At that point, you will be in a traffic circle, so stay in your left lane but beware of oncoming traffic. Don't worry, you have the right-of-way. Stay in the circle, and then you will see an exit on your right …"

By this time, I felt like he was speaking another language. I still felt the same as I did when I walked in—lost.

He continued, "Then take that right, follow it, and then the road will curve but stay on it. Don't exit. Then you will be on a long bridge. Stay on it until it ends. Then go up to the second traffic light, hang a right, and you will be at your destination."

Am I supposed to remember all that? I thought. I asked the guy, "Do you know any road signs or something I can follow so I know if I'm on the right track?"

"No, sorry man, don't know any road signs. I just know how to get there?"

At that point, I didn't have any other choice but to trust that this guy knew what he was talking about. At least he sounded convincing.

"OK, so can you run those instructions by me again?" I asked. This time I was willing to pay more attention.

He started over. "You go down this road, make a right …" Five to ten minutes later, I jumped back into the car.

"Did you get directions?" my colleague asked.

"Yep."

"Can I see them? Did you write them down?"

"Nope, we just have to go this way," I said.

Sure enough, as I followed his instructions the way I heard them, we arrived at our destination. What was so amazing was, though it was an unconventional approach in the way he gave me directions, the route to the manufacturing plant was exactly how this guy described it. I basically had to follow his voice that I could hear in my head.

When we're not sure of how to get to where we are going, and the map isn't clear, we have to rely on the voice of the Holy Spirit in real time. Even if we know the destination, following the voice of God is paramount. Now-a-days, because of technology, we don't always have to stop and ask for directions. We have tools like a GPS to help us get where we need to go.

The third tool God left us to help navigate our course toward fulfilling our call is a spiritual GPS—His Voice. God gave us the Holy Spirit to lead us and to guide us into all truth.

A Dedicated GPS

I recently purchased a GPS (Global Positioning System) and used it on a trip to Washington D.C. It was interesting how it worked. Because it's a navigational tool (a receiver which communicates with satellites), all I had to do was type in the address to where I was going and let the GPS do the rest. The machine gave me step-by-step directions by visually displaying the route, street names, and exits on a little screen about the size of the palm of my hand. It also provided the same instructions via an audible voice that literally prompted me when and where to turn.

What I found amazing was whenever I took a wrong turn, it immediately responded, "Recalculating, recalculating." Then it determined my current position on the road and where I got off course relative to my destination. As a result, it recalculated my position and gave me directions on what turns to take next, to get me back on course. Even though I lost some time, the GPS continued to give me directions until I arrived at my destination.

That's what the Holy Spirit does when we get off course. He immediately and gently lets us know, "You just made a wrong turn!" Isaiah 30:21 says you will hear God's voice instructing you "whenever you turn to the right or to the left." In other words, the Holy Spirit will instruct us all along the way.

And like a GPS, God recalculates. The Spirit of God takes into account where we are, at what point we got off track, and will either get us to turn around or re-route us down another path that intersects with our main route, to get us back on course. When we're in love with God, He can take any mistake, road block, and detour in life, and make it all work together for our good (see Romans 8:28). God can even help us make up for lost time.

If we're willing to follow His voice, God is willing to get us back on track, if necessary, but we have to recognize when God is speaking. In John 10, Jesus said that we are His sheep, and that we know His voice, which is distinct from the voice of a stranger. We will cover more about recognizing God's voice in chapter 14.

When I mentioned asking the city worker for directions to the manufacturing plant, the instructions didn't make sense. What he said wasn't logical, because the guy couldn't tell me any road signs or exits. Still I learned that day that faith is not based on logic, it's based on obedience. When we are willing to follow God's will, it doesn't matter if we can see the road signs or not. No matter how illogical it may be, God promises to lead us every step of the way by His Spirit. Our job is to go after our call with all our might. If we come to a fork in the road, we don't have to ask a stranger like Alice did with the Cheshire cat. God left us with a map, a compass, and a GPS. As long as we follow Him, He won't steer us wrong.

Chapter 12
7 Principles

1. If we're willing to ask, God is ready to show us. But be prepared, we may only get a glimpse, a nugget, or a thought of what's next. Oftentimes, God will share in phases, because He wants us to walk by faith, one step at a time.

2. God never intended for any of us to venture out in life without guidance. Otherwise, we'd risk making wrong turns and decisions, resulting in costly delays or even worse, missing our destination.

3. When we acknowledge the travel professional of life, God our Creator, who knows what's best for us, we make room for Him to direct our steps and to keep us on that well-defined route.

4. Just as an empire keeps harmony in a baseball game, God's peace keeps harmony in our hearts by taking two opposing wills—our will and His will—and joining them together.

5. To trust God means to entrust our future, our life, and our calling into His hands, and believe Him to keep His word to us.

6. When we're not sure of how to get to where we are going, and the map isn't clear, we have to rely on the voice of the Holy Spirit in real time.

7. And like a GPS, God recalculates. The Spirit of God takes into account where we are and at what point we got off track and will either get us to turn around or will re-route us down another path that intersects with our main route, to get us back on course.

THE SEVENTH DIMENSION: IT'S ALL ABOUT GOD'S TIMING

CHAPTER 13

TIMING IS CRITICAL TO SUCCESS

To everything there is a season, a time for every purpose under heaven.
—Ecclesiastes 3:1 NKJV

IT WAS ONLY three minutes after takeoff from LaGuardia airport that the US Airways Flight 1549 had a shocking encounter; they struck a flock of Canadian geese during their ascent. Seconds later, the control tower heard the captain's response, "Hit birds. We've lost thrust on both engines."[1]

With engine failure, the crew of flight 1549 had limited options. They considered turning back to LaGuardia, but with no engines, they couldn't. Also, they considered an emergency landing to the neighboring New Jersey's airport, but that was out of the question as well. Captain Sullenberger (aka captain Sully), the captain of flight 1549, described his assessment of the situation by saying, "Based on my experience and looking out the window, I could tell by the altitude and decent rate that neither [airport] was a viable option. I also thought that I could not afford to choose wrongly ... landing short, even by a little bit, could have catastrophic consequences."[2] Captain Sully had to make a different, quick, and decisive decision. "We're gonna be in the Hudson," he announced to the control tower.[3]

Despite engine failure, the captain and his team successfully glided the plane into the Hudson River, all within six minutes after flight takeoff.[4] This miraculous landing is known as the "Miracle on the Hudson." All 155 passengers and crew members survived. Captain Sully and his crew were praised as heroes. His split second decision, at the right time, made all the difference between life and death. Timing was key to everyone's success and survival.

Our experiences may or may not be as extreme as the Flight 1549 situation, but that miraculous landing illustrates a valuable principle specifically related to our call: Timing is critical in fulfilling it. The right time is when God's purposes and desires converge with our obedience to produce His eternal results. Our pursuit of God's timing represents the Seventh Dimension to Fulfilling The Call.

Your Timing Affects Your Calling

Ecclesiastes 3:1 states, "To everything there is a season, a time for every purpose under heaven."[5] This verse points out that for every God-ordained activity, He gives us time to realize it. Additionally, there are three characteristics of time that impact our call.

The first characteristic of time is that time can be defined as fixed or appointed. It's a set time. A simple way to illustrate this unique aspect of time is to consider our birthday. It comes around at a set time every year. Heaven recorded our birth, and we can't change it because it's a fixed day. Similarly, God has a fixed or set time for us to do what He's called us to do.

Previously in chapter 1, I mentioned that God had to build Abraham's and Sarah's faith, so they could believe to receive the promise to become the progenitor of nations. At one point along their faith journey, and because of their age and Sarah's infertility, they got tired of waiting. It was hard to believe for the many that God had promised would be their descendants, when in fact, they were struggling to believe God for the one baby they still didn't have.

In Genesis, 16:2, Sarah voiced here complaint to Abraham and said, "See now, the LORD has restrained me from bearing children."[6] Restrain is equivalent to being held back. Her feeling of being held back from bearing children translates to her struggle with God's timing. We often feel the same way when we don't see things happening as fast as we want them to. These struggles make us second-guess God's promises. In reality, sometimes we struggle with God's timing.

The irony is this: When God makes a promise, He delivers on time. Our calendars, clocks, or deadlines do not drive heaven. God is Eternal, and He has His own timetable based on His eternal purpose.

Eventually, God sent an angel to Abraham and Sarah to get them on the same schedule. In Genesis 18:14, He told them, "Is anything too hard for Jehovah? At the set time I will return unto thee, when the season cometh round, and Sarah shall have a son."[7] This conveys to me that God had a fixed point in time for Isaac's birth. Likewise, God has a set time to fulfill His promises in our lives.

God's Opportune Time

The second characteristic of time is that time can be opportune. I experienced an occasion like this when it was time for me to leave the retail store I talked about earlier in chapter five. It had been three years since my decision to go to college full time. I submitted my application for the third time. Both times previously, I had been accepted, but my finances just didn't agree. This time however, my mind was made up. I had to do it; I had to start. I sensed the time was now, and it was getting closer to the end of the registration period.

It took me weeks to write my letter of resignation from work. It was a hard decision to leave, especially since I had been working in this store for so long. I had my letter ready to hand in when I went to work that evening. I had to see Mr. C and personally hand him my letter. Oddly enough, Mr. C left word with my supervisor for me to come and see him when I clocked in. *Wow.* I thought, *God must be pushing me so I don't' change my mind or something.*

When I walked into Mr. C's office, I glanced across the room. His desk was organized and filled with papers. On his wall were portraits of his wife and family. On the back of his credenza, he still had the artwork I gave him many years ago for Father's Day. He was more than a store manager to me; he was like a coach.

"Hello, how are you this evening?" he asked.

"I'm good," I responded hesitantly. I didn't know why he called me into his office, but I knew why I needed to speak to him.

"Mr. C, I'm glad you called me in because I needed to see you anyhow."

"Have a seat," he responded.

Mr. C. started, "As you know, our company is going through a major restructuring."

"I'm aware of that, but I'm not sure how that relates to me."

"Well, your job has been eliminated." He paused then continued, "We're offering you two choices. You can take a

TIMING IS CRITICAL TO SUCCESS

lower paid position and remain employed with us, or you can take this severance package that includes a lump some check of over $3,500. If you take the package, your last day with the company will be two weeks from today."

Wait a minute, I thought. *That's when I have to be on campus to find a place to stay.* I tried to maintain my composure as much as I could. My resignation letter was in my hands, and I was standing there listening to how the company actually wanted to pay me to leave? *Are you kidding?* I thought. Fireworks were going off in my head. *Of course, I'll take the money! This was exactly the push I needed to go off to college!*

"I'll take the severance package," I said humbly. I quietly slipped my prepared resignation letter into my back pocket.

"Did you still need to see me?" he asked.

"No sir," I responded. "Thank you."

As I walked out of his office and turned the corner to head to the stock room, I realized, "I could pay my deposit, finish my enrollment, buy my books, and more!"

That was just the beginning of the financial blessings that started rolling in. In fact, three weeks later, I received another check in the mail for over $2,500, as result of leaving that particular company. It was God's opportune time for me.

An "opportune time" means the right time or the best time to do something. For example, when would be the best time for someone to throw you a surprise birthday party, six months after your birthday, or two months prior? Of course, there are exceptions, but you'd probably agree that the ideal time would be on your birthday, as this timing most likely would have a positive impact and be the most meaningful.

In the New Testament, the Greek word for this unique aspect of time is kairos, which means space of time or opportunity. Dr. Folz's book, *For Such a Time As This*, describes kairos as a special time when God arranges all the details in order. Then He opens the door and gives us the opportunity to go along with Him in what He's about to accomplish.[8] How well synchronized we are with God's timing determines are effectiveness in executing our call.

When God opens a kairos moment for us, a window of opportunity, we have to grab it. I had to seize that opportunity to leave my job and go back to college. If I had stayed with that company, I'm not sure how much longer it would have taken for me to position myself to go back to college full-time. It could have taken months or perhaps years. Taking that severance package was God's kairos moment to push me forward toward what He was calling me to.

To seize a God-ordained opportunity, we may incur risks. When we're called to do great exploits, risks can be expected but don't worry, God has our back. Also, the benefits will far outweigh the sacrifices. God has called each of us to walk by faith, so we must be bold, confident, and on the lookout for the payoff.

Our diligence will create opportunities. John Maxwell, author of, *The 21 Most Powerful Minutes in a Leader's Day,* states that when you "determine to seize a right opportunity despite the risk, you build momentum for the next opportunity that comes your way."[9] When we step through one door, another one will open. We must not pull back or procrastinate but be willing and determined to capture the moment. The opportune moment will pay dividends.

To clutch an opportunity, we must do it quickly. In John 9:4, Jesus expressed, "All of us must quickly carry out the tasks assigned us by the one who sent me, for there is little time left before the night falls and all work comes to an end."[10] In other words, it's important to quickly take action while the window is open and before the door of opportunity closes. But remember, we can't move ahead of God or lag behind. Timing is essential.

God's Time Takes Preparation

After the experience of flight 1549, the National Transportation Safety Board (NTSB) tried to replicate the event with flight simulators to see if there were better options than landing in the Hudson River. During these simulations, the four pilots who were tested successfully landed back at LaGuardia airport, but with one caveat built into the simulations, and that was "knowing in advance that they were going to suffer a bird strike and that the engine could not be restarted."[11] However, "When the NTSB later imposed a 30 second delay before they could respond, in recognition that it wasn't reasonable to expect a pilot to assess the situation and react instantly, all four pilots crashed."[12]

Knowing exactly what to expect, initially made those pilots successful during the simulations. But you know as well as I do that life is not preprogrammed and neither is the calling on our life. We are involved in a daily faith walk, and preparation can make all the difference in the world as to whether we succeed or fail.

For Captain Sully, preparation enabled him to succeed when opportunity presented itself, although the opportunity was in the form of a crisis. The flight simulation tests proved that he made the right decision at a critical time. Preparation embodied in all his training and experiences allowed him to rely on instinct and make the right decisions. Captain Sully summarized it this way, "Everything I had done in my career had some way been a preparation for that moment … in some way contributed to the outcome."[13]

Are you waiting on God to explode with something big in your life? Are you sitting around waiting on God? There is no better time than now to prepare. Mike Murdock asserts, "Champions do not become champions in the ring. They are merely recognized in the ring. Their becoming, happens in their daily routine."[14]

Preparation sets us up for success. Doing the groundwork now prepares us for opportune times. It allows us to be optimally productive when God shows up. There is a saying that says "it's better to be prepared and not have an opportunity, than to have an opportunity and not be prepared." Preparation embraces opportunity. Preparation reduces risk.

Seasonal Changes

> "As long as the earth endures, seedtime and harvest, cold and heat, summer and winter, and day and night will not cease."
> —Genesis 8:22 HCSB

According to Genesis, man became so wicked that God used a worldwide flood to destroy all living beings that walked on the surface of the earth, but He spared Noah and his family and a selection of animals because Noah pleased God.

After the flood, God made a two-fold promise. First, He promised to never flood the whole earth again. Secondly, He promised that as long as the earth existed, cold and heat, seedtime and harvest, day and night, summer and winter would never end. God reestablished the cycle of time and seasons, so that humanity and nature could flourish.

Ever since humanity's second chance from God, man has come to appreciate the value of time and seasons. Man learned to follow the pattern of the sun (from sunrise to sunset) and the moon cycle, eventually learning to track the seasons. In fact, studying the sky became the basis for tracking time in the same way that we use our calendars and clocks today. According to the National Geographic experts:

> The moon cycle gave the ancients a way to track a small amount of time, the month. But then they began to notice longer patterns, like the seasons. They saw how star formations and alignments moved, and they could time these movements with seasonal changes.
> Our planet spins around on an axis that is offset by about twenty-four degrees. During the summer, the axis is angled toward the sun. More sunlight means hotter temperatures. It also means that we get a certain view of the sky ... but as earth continues in its orbit, the axis tilts away from the sun. That's what gives us winter and different views of the sky.
> This cycle proceeds like clockwork, which is what made it so handy for our ancestors. Developing the concept of seasons by looking at the patterns of the stars, put them more in tune with their environment and allowed them to plan for hunting and gathering and all the other activities needed in order to survive. The ability to predict changes in the environment meant our ancestors could adapt. By adapting, they thrived.[15]

Seasons represent the third characteristic of time, showing that time can be a fixed period. When our ancestors learned to recognize the seasons, they learned to adapt to drastic climatic changes. Adaptation was paramount to their survival. In the same way, spiritual, seasonal changes affect our call. Following God's plan for our life means that changes in the spiritual climate are inevitable. This Seventh Dimension of our call requires that we adapt to these changes so we can thrive.

Different Seasons, Different Activities

> May the name of God be praised forever and ever, for wisdom and power belong to Him. He changes the times and the seasons.
> —Daniel 2:20–21 HCSB

Also, this fixed period of time determines what special activities will take place. Your birthday may be during the winter season or perhaps around springtime. The season of your birth may affect how you celebrate your birthday. If you were born during the summer, your celebration may be an outdoor event, such as, a birthday party in the park. However, if your birthday is during the extreme cold months of winter, you may opt to celebrate it with more of an indoor activity, such as, a home gathering or a visit to your favorite restaurant. The season determines the activity.

Nature further highlights this principle of seasonal change. The earth has four seasons—spring, summer, fall, and winter. These seasons last for a fixed period of time, and based on these different seasons, nature takes on different activities. Like nature, we must ensure we're doing the right things, as we transition through our seasons.

God launches us into different phases of our lives so we can accomplish certain things at certain times. God's set time for us will influence the seasons and will determine the opportunities that come our way.

Spring Forth

Springtime represents a time of renewal and rebirth. Because of warmer temperatures than are experienced in winter, plants spring up. Flowers bloom, and birds sing, while other animals wake up from their winter sleep and begin being active.

During this season of our lives, God wants to do something new in us and for us. According to Isaiah, God tells us, "See, I am doing a new thing! Now it springs up; do you not perceive it? I am making a way in the desert and streams in the wasteland."[16]

Your spring season can represent something new in you, like a new relationship, starting a new venture, going back to school, or getting involved in a new area of ministry. The springtimes of our lives are times of breaking ground toward something new.

Spring is also associated with a time of sowing, as farmers plant their seeds. It's during this time, God wants us to sow into what He has for us. Whether it's sowing into a ministry, our families, our relationships, our education, or our gifts and talents, it's a season of sowing. God wants us to sow our time, energy, resources, and sometimes our money. Whatever seeds God puts in our hands, we must sow it into our destiny.

And with spring comes rain. As a kid I often heard, "April showers bring May flowers." I guess that depended on what part of country you lived in. The emphasis of this statement was the rain's productivity. Isaiah 55:10 tells us that the purpose for the rain is "watering the earth and making it bud and flourish, so that it yields seed."[17] Ideally, God showers His blessings, favor, and resources into our lives so the new thing He's doing in us can take root.

Spring is also a season of inclement weather, such as, lighting storms. Spiritually speaking, these springtime storms come to test and challenge the new thing God is doing. They come to make us doubt what God is doing for us, as we try to break ground. Knowing this, we must hold fast to God's Word and keep sowing, because if we hold on, we will see the benefits. Galatians 6:9 reminds us, "So don't get tired of doing what is good. Don't get discouraged and give up, for we will reap a harvest of blessing at the appropriate time."[18]

Productive Season

After spring, comes the hottest season of the year—summertime. Summer also has the longest days and shortest nights of the year. Summer is when nature experiences continual, consistent growth. Also, people have a tendency to spend more time enjoying outside activities, like playtime, yard work, outdoor vacations, festivals, events in the park, etc. We can accomplish more things outdoors in the summer than in any other season.

Relating to our call, the summer of our lives is the opportunity to be the most productive. It's during our summers that God wants to stabilize what was birthed in the springtime of our lives. This is when our gifts and talents consistently produce results. As I stated previously, Jesus encouraged us to work while it's day. In the Greek, "day" literally means a space of time between dawn and dark. So in this season, God gives us a space in time to produce and stabilize what He placed in us.

Harvest Time

Fall, also known as autumn, is the next season in line. Fall is a time of transition, as nature transitions from summer to winter. Trees change in color, animals gather their food, and birds begin to migrate toward warmer climates. Nature makes preparation for the upcoming cold season. Our days become shorter. Fall is also a time of harvest, a time of reaping. When we are faithful to cultivating the seed God planted in us, God will mature it. He will cause a harvest time so we can reap the benefits of our labor.

TIMING IS CRITICAL TO SUCCESS

Some years ago, God took us through a type of fall season of our lives—a season of transition. Our oldest son was about ten years old, and we purchased a small, cheap, electric piano at a garage sale. During this phase of his life, he was very interested in sports, so I, like most fathers, focused on developing his sporting skills and aspirations. The piano was just another collectible in his room, along with other toys and electronics, or so I thought. When he wasn't playing, practicing sports, or studying for school, he was banging on that little piano. He would diligently spend hours playing on that piano, which had only had one consistent sound to me—noise. This went on for over five years.

One day, a few months before Christmas of that year, a friend of ours paid us a visit. She brought along her Yamaha keyboard. She played a few songs and talked awhile. At the end of her visit, as we were sitting at the kitchen table chatting, my son came downstairs and saw her keyboard.

"May I try out your keyboard?" he asked.

"Sure," she responded.

He grabbed the keyboard from its leaning position against the wall, laid it on the sofa, plugged it in, then dropped to his knees and started playing.

I was shocked. When I heard the sound that was coming out of that keyboard, my mouth dropped open!

What!?! I thought. The melodic sound, the chords, the music was incredible. "I did not know you could play!" I screamed.

"Oh yeah dad, if I only had a real keyboard, I could do something with it."

Well, guess what he got just two months later for Christmas? Yes, a real, professional grade keyboard. The rest is history. Today he is an incredible musician. Incidentally, music, not sports, is his first love.

7 DIMENSIONS TO FULFILLING YOUR CALL

The moral of this story is that my son sowed into his gift. He practiced hour upon hour on that little garage sale piano that to me only had one sound, but all along, God was cultivating his musical gift. He developed a musical ear and trained his fingers to play chords. Because of his faithfulness, he's reaping a harvest of becoming a skilled musician. It's the new thing God starts in the spring season and cultivates during the summer that He will leverage into our future.

Winter's Wake Up Call

It was my first job after moving to Virginia. My first few weeks seemed somewhat satisfying. I met a lot of new people, both coworkers and customers. I also spent days absorbing everything I could: work assignments, policies and guidelines, products and services, customer locations, new tools, and tips about repairing equipment. My days were full.

Unfortunately, I was the new kid on the block. I had a lot to learn. It wasn't like my previous job where I was productive, had consistent flow, was considered a veteran, and knew so much I was on cruise control. Now I was trying to find my way in this new company, trying to fit in, and starting all over to establish a name for myself.

After returning from work one of those early evenings, I sat on the bed exhausted from the day, and yet on the inside, was still restless. I was adjusting. I was used to a little bit more than just going straight home from work, but I was starting all over again and this time without all the responsibilities and the demands of ministry.

Previously, I wore multiple hats, working full-time for an oil company while in ministry as finance director, minister, musician, and holding down other roles at our home church. And if that wasn't enough, I was involved in my own music ministry, and I was a husband and father of a new family when I had time. I felt like I was riding on a merry-go-round, and I didn't know how to get off. Then one day, God began to blow the wind of change my direction.

I wondered how I got there. Everything in my life came to a complete halt. I felt like God had His finger on me, and I couldn't move, yet internally, my motor was still running. I thought, *God, I'm going out of my mind sitting still!*

Not understanding what God was doing, one day my brother called and shared with me a phenomenal dream God had given him. In the dream, he saw two trees that represented my wife and me in the blight of winter with no leaves, only branches. He continued to tell me that even though it appeared nothing was happening on the outside—everything around us appeared to have died—there was something happening that you couldn't see on the surface. God was doing something in us. Our roots were growing deeper and deeper into the ground. Though the outward seemed barren, on the inside, we were being restored. That's when I began to realize that we were at a different season of our lives. We were in winter, and I had to accept the process that God was taking us through.

Winter is nature's time of dormancy. Trees are barren and for most plants, growth stops and some die. Some animals hibernate during this time even though others have migrated. It's during the winter months, we experience the shortest days of the year and longer nights. It's a time of inactivity, as the climate is not conducive for bearing fruit.

It is during these times of spiritual, winter inactivity that I feel most of us struggle because nothing appears to be happening. Emotionally, we may feel like questioning God, asking things like, "Where are You" and "Have You abandoned me?" On the contrary, God promised never to leave us; He is always there. Psalm 30:5 described it this way: "Weeping may endure for a night, but joy comes in the morning."[19] The writer of this Psalm used the cycle of days to describe our breakthrough. If we transpose that verse using the cycle of seasons, then night would represent winter and morning would represent spring. So the reason why we can endure the winter is because it won't last forever. Springtime is coming again; it's just around the corner.

Furthermore, it may be hard to believe, but winter is a time of evolution in areas of your life that you may not see. Believe me, God is doing something deep within you. It may not be tangible at the time, but He's preparing things He will call for at a later time. I mentioned already that some plants die during winter, but what's interesting, is when they die, some leave their seeds behind.[20] These seeds produce new life when spring rolls around again.

In my front yard, I had three small trees. However, one of those trees seemed to transition from green to brown to no leaves, rather early. One day my neighbor, the one who built the add-on to his house, hired a contractor to cut down a few trees in his backyard. He came over to me and said, "You need to cut that tree down; it's dead. I'll send my contractor over to cut it down for you."

I looked up at the tree and thought for a moment. "No thank you," I responded. "I'll leave it be." My thought was that it may look dead, but I believed there was still life in it.

Some months later when spring rolled around again, I stepped out my front door, and I noticed that tree that my neighbor thought was on its last leg. It was blooming with green leaves again.

Then God showed me that our dreams and visions sometimes become like my tree that appeared to have died. It's OK; we just have to endure the winter. Patience through the winter is necessary for our calling because there are some things God wants to remove from our lives, and there are seeds of vision, passion, and wisdom that He wants to resurrect in us. And like that tree, He will bring life again.

Habakkuk 2:3 tells us that though the vision seems like it's never going to come and winter will never end, just wait. Be patient. Even waiting is like being in winter. Only God knows how long winter will last. But in the end, your dream is going to break through, and your calling will be fulfilled.

In God's Time, It's Beautiful

Another purpose for the winter season is related to fruit. Winter is nature's way of cleansing and revitalizing itself. It also helps to determine the quality of fruit on fruit trees when the time does come for the fruit to ripen. John 15:2 speaks of how we are like branches, and God will prune us so that we can bear the fruit that He's looking for. When a tree is pruned, the diseased and dead parts are cut away so that the tree can be more fruitful and flourishing. Look at winter as a time for pruning. This pruning process is God's way of removing out of our lives any hindrances to our fruitfulness.

Psalm 1 affirms that God is looking for each of us to bear fruit in our season. Bishop Jakes comments, "There is fruit that is buried within you. You can produce it effectively and powerfully, but only in your season."[21] God is looking for fruit based on the seeds He has planted; seeds that coincide with what He has called us to do.

Ecclesiastes 3:11 conveys to us that God made everything beautiful for our lives in its time. In God's time, what we are called to do will be suitable, it will fit, and it will come together. And the entire set of activities centered in that season of our life and calling will be appropriate for our maturity so we can bear the fruit He's looking for.

The focus here is God's time, not our time. When it's the right time, then "nothing can be added to it or taken from it."[22] God is able to do "far more than we would ever dare to ask or even dream of."[23]

God will use the seasons to prepare us, to birth new life through us, to mature us, and to remove out of us, that which hinders us from being fruitful. Knowing God's timing is key to enable us to successfully accomplish the call in our life. Understanding the seasons we're in provides hope and insight, knowing that God is active on our behalf. Because different seasons require different activities, we must look to God to give us the wisdom we need, because it's He who determines our time and our seasons.

Chapter 13

7 Principles

1. The right time is upon us when God's purposes and desires converge with our obedience to produce His eternal results.

2. Heaven recorded our birth, and we can't change it because that's a fixed time. Similarly, God has a fixed or set time for us to do what He's called us to do.

3. When we're called to do great exploits, and all of us are, risks are to be expected; but there's no cause for worry because God has our back.

4. Doing the groundwork now, prepares us for opportune times and allows us to be the most productive as we can possibly be when God shows up.

5. God's set time for us will influence the seasons and will determine the opportunities that come our way.

6. It may be hard to believe, but winter is a time of evolution in areas of our lives that we may not see. God is doing something deep within us. It may not be tangible at the time, but He's preparing things He will call for at a later time.

7. God will use the seasons to prepare us, to birth new life in us, to mature us, and to remove out of us, that which hinders us from being fruitful.

CHAPTER 14

PROPER DISCERNMENT

Teach me good discernment and knowledge, for I believe in your commandments.
—Psalm 119:66 NAU

WHAT IF WHAT I'm sensing is wrong? But if I don't act, I might miss God, I thought. But if I end this now, why would that be considered an opportunity?

For several days, it was challenging, thinking about what I had to do that night. I felt like I was in a dentist chair, overly anxious, waiting for the dentist to return with that dreaded needle.

These were my comrades, and they believed in me. Was I letting them down? I deliberated.

We'd been together as a music team for some years, and we'd been friends longer than that. We had traveled together and had broke bread together; we'd been together through thick and thin. Because of all the gatherings and outdoor events, I didn't want to be wrong. Oddly enough, every time I decided against what I had to share that night, I didn't feel

PROPER DISCERNMENT

right. And yet at the same time, I felt like something was being taken from me, and I was mourning. Perhaps the root of my struggle was an unwillingness to let go.

The drive to the church typically took about twenty minutes, but oddly enough, seconds felt like minutes, and minutes felt like hours. Even though I was early, I saw several cars in the parking lot. This time, they were exceptionally early. It was like they knew; perhaps something was in the air. Unfortunately, this didn't make my decision any easier.

When I walked into the sanctuary, there was a joyful ambiance. I paused to look around. Everybody was in his or her place. The musicians were warming up with a festive song. The pianist was playing soulfully. The syncopation of the drummer and rhythmic sound of the bass guitarist followed along.

The sound man had a few of the singers checking the microphones, while the rest of the ladies were sitting across from each other chatting. Some of the guys in the tenor section exploded into laughter, obviously glad to see each other after a long day on the job. What was on my heart was weighing so heavily on me that I felt like I was carrying a rain cloud, and I was about to drench this joyful atmosphere.

Why was it so difficult? I kept asking myself. The irony was that I was hoping in some way I'd get a reply that could change my mind.

I couldn't delay any longer. I walked onto the stage and grabbed a microphone. "Everyone, thanks for being here tonight. I have an announcement to make." Almost immediately, everything stopped. There was no music and no chatter; all eyes were focused on me. It was so quiet that you could actually hear the silence.

"This next event will be our last one together. I'm discontinuing our music ministry."

The silence became a crescendo! Like winning a championship when the team dumps a bucket of iced Gatorade on their coach, I could see the cold rush of my announcement envelop the group. Everybody was taken aback. Even I had to catch my own breath. I couldn't believe the words that had come out of my mouth.

Their faces expressed the sadness that filled my heart. I was at a loss for words. Then suddenly, I felt a blanket of peace cover me. It was the right thing to do. I didn't know why God was leading me this way or what He had in store. I just knew that if I acted on what I was sensing, then in some way, God would make everything turn out fine.

Transition

This took place in November that year. Two months later, I received a letter from my job that the company had decided to shut down our division, and I needed to look for a new job. Little did I know that exactly four months later from the date when I announced the end of our music ministry, I would start a new job in another state. This is how our relocation to Virginia got started.

I learned a valuable lesson from that experience, which I believe is important to the pursuit of our call. I learned the importance of discernment. I had to distinguish God's voice from all the noise around me, making sure I heard and understood what He was speaking into my life.

Jesus told the Pharisees that they could discern the sky, but they couldn't discern the times. They could tell when it was going to rain or even predict a storm, but they couldn't discern the change in the spiritual climate. Jesus stood right in front of them, but they were so religious that they missed the opportunity to encounter the Messiah for whom they had been waiting.

In Psalm 16:11, David said that God would show us the path of life. While going down the distinct paths God has for us, we need to remember that our paths have turns. Knowing when to turn, which path to take, and at what juncture in our lives, takes discernment.

Godly discernment will enable us to know the difference between what's OK for us as compared to what is God's best for us. It aids us to know God's will, God's timing, and our season. In John 10:27, Jesus said, "My sheep know my voice." When we are sensitive to God's voice, our spiritual GPS begins with the process of discernment.

My change in jobs represented a change in the spiritual climate for my life. Like the decision I had to make concerning our music ministry, little did I know, that months later I would end up living in another state. However, God knew, but I had to recognize what God was speaking. I needed discernment related to my transition. I had to distinguish God's will and timing for my life. Discernment is drastically important in fulfilling our call, and it's a critical ingredient contained within this Seventh Dimension which is All About God's Timing.

The Importance of Proper Discernment

First Chronicles 12 describes the skill of David's mighty men. After David was anointed king over Israel in Hebron, the writer began to describe the type of men that came from everywhere to support David. As part of their description, their skill in the art of combat warfare was described. Some were skillful with a sword, others with the bow and arrow. Some were skillful with the left hand, as well as, the right hand. There was one who slew a giant and another who slew a lion in a pit on a snowy day. All the different tribes of Israel were described as skillful in various areas of warfare fighting.

However, there was one group of people who had an unusual skill, the tribe of Issachar. Their skill was not described in terms of the ability to handle a spear or sword, but rather, they had the ability to discern the times and to know what Israel should do. They understood Israel's purpose, they understood Israel's season, and they understood Israel's timing.

What is Discernment?

Discernment means to separate thoroughly. It's the ability to consider a situation and thoroughly separate mind and heart. In addition, it means to recognize and distinguish. To recognize the good verses the bad, the right way verses the wrong way, and the good verses the best. It is being able to tell when it's time and when it's not. Discernment is making the right judgment about a situation so that we can make the right decision.

Dr. Charles Stanley defines discernment as "the ability to see beyond the appearance of our circumstances, perceive God's viewpoint on them, and make wise judgments in response."[1]

Sometimes the whole picture is not clear, and at times, it's hard to know what's at the end of the road. Initially, it wasn't clear to me why I had to discontinue the music ministry, but God enabled me to see His viewpoint on the matter. Even though I didn't see the whole picture, at least God showed me the next step.

The Call Sets Boundaries

If you have ever traveled by air, you know that the airline industry sets your destination in advance. Based on where we're going and what city we're leaving from, they create a flight itinerary. This itinerary identifies our travel date, departure time, and arrival time to our destination.

God has determined the flight plan for each of us. Based on where God is taking us, He lays out the "call" itinerary. He determines the scope of what we're called to do. He determines the destination, and even the resources and provisions are preset.

According to Genesis 37, God wanted Joseph in Egypt, so He initiated Joseph's flight plan. Psalm 105:17 further states, "He sent Joseph as a slave to Egypt to save his people from starvation."[2] The calling on Joseph's life was summoning him to this foreign land. The change in the spiritual climate commenced when Jacob sent Joseph to go check on his brothers. This was God's way of setting Joseph's departure date: destination—Egypt.

His brothers were taking care of the flock in a place called Shechem, about three days' journey from where they lived in Hebron. But the brothers eventually moved to Dothan, adding another day's journey. Why? Because God had to make sure Joseph caught his connecting flight from Dothan, which is where his brothers sold him as a slave to a caravan of Ishmaelites who were on their way to Egypt.

Distinguishing God's Boundaries

Built into the airline flight plan are inherent limitations to our destination so that we arrive safe and on time. In the same way, God sets boundaries within our "call" itinerary for the following three reasons:

1. To ensure we get to the right destination. For instance, layovers may be included in our flight plan to make sure we catch the right connecting

flight. Sometimes, layovers are included in our "call" itinerary. For example, we may start in New York, but if God wants us in Arizona, hang on. Along the way, we might have a scheduled layover in Florida (for a few years) because there is something there for us to do. Joseph even had a few layovers (Potiphar's house and prison) on his way to actually fulfilling his dream of ruling.

Also, the airline ticket we hold won't let us on just any flight, but we are constrained to a designated flight so we don't end up in the wrong city. Likewise, God places restrictions on our itinerary to ensure we don't end up off course. In other words, within God's will, we have limitless potential and unlimited grace. Every detail of our life will come together, because we are called to do specific things, for specific people, in specific places, all for specific purposes. However, outside of His will, there are restraints.

The book of Acts tells the story of how God set a boundary for Paul. In Paul's "call" itinerary, he was limited from going to Asia during his missionary journey (see Acts 16:6). The Holy Spirit would not release him to go because God set this boundary. Why did God limit where Paul would travel in advance? Could it be that the trip could have been detrimental to his ministry? Was his life in danger? Or perhaps God wanted him somewhere else. It could have been that God already had that area mapped as part of someone else's calling to fulfill. We see later that God definitely wanted Paul in Macedonia, not Asia. Discerning both the destination and restrictions are important to our calling.

2. To ensure we stay synchronized with Him. God limited how He wanted Joseph to gain an audience

with Pharaoh. At one point, Joseph was challenged with discerning God's will and timing, as he tried to get on a different flight plan to get out of prison. In Genesis 40:14, he told chief butler, "Make mention of me to Pharaoh, and get me out of this house."[3] Straightway, the chief butler forgot him. Joseph wanted out, but it was not time to stop doing what he had been called to do—to serve in prison. Joseph was off pace with God's timing.

We often feel the same way. When things don't seem to be going our way, we feel that God has forgotten us. During these times, it's important to discern God's voice so we don't get out of step with what He is doing.

In spite of it all, Joseph didn't stop serving, but rather, he stayed productive. Even the jailer let Joseph run everything because he could see that the favor and prosperity of God was on him. If we discern God's time correctly, even in difficulty, like Joseph, we can continue to be productive when we are in our calling.

3. To keep us focused. If we're not careful, sometimes because of our giftings, we're tempted to do things God has not called us to do. While some may not know when to say no, there are some who are influenced to go beyond what God has intended. It's easy to forget that we have physical limitations. Bishop Jakes comments that sometimes when we're motivated to impress or gain the accolades of others, we take on too much and fail to reach the goal or crash because we ignored our limitations.[4]

As part of the body of Christ, we can't be all parts all at once. Trying to be all things to all people can be overwhelming and cause a deficit in our relationship with God. There are only twenty-four hours in a day, and yet, sometimes we strive as if there were twenty-five. That's why God limits us in advance and sets the boundaries. For everything within His boundaries, there is grace. Outside of them, we are dependent on His mercy.

Barriers to Discernment

One day I was driving home after running a few errands. The car in the lane to my left was extremely nice looking; it was a deep gray, four-door BMW. My old Toyota Camry had some obvious wear and tear and could have used a fresh paint job to even try to compare to that illustrious shine this BMW had, but "so what" I thought. The elegant look was not that important to me. I had finally paid my car loan off some week's prior. This Camry was mine. And because of that, I cherished it.

I was listening to some teaching tapes. I was relaxing and couldn't wait to get home.

I just felt this impression to look to my left, and that's when I noticed something odd about this nice looking car. It was ahead of me by about two to three feet, driving the same direction. But then I could tell the car was starting to veer to the right, right into my lane!

"Hey! I shouted as I blew my horn." Immediately, the car swerved back into his original lane.

Wow! I thought. *Wasn't it obvious, I was right here?*

Then it dawned on me that perhaps he didn't see me. I must have been in his blind spot.

A blind spot occurs when the person driving his vehicle can't see accurately, an approaching vehicle in the next lane they want to merge into, because the angle of the side mirrors inhibits his visibility. If not careful, blind spots can be dangerous for both drivers.

The Old Testament talks about a prophet named Balaam who experienced what I would call a blind spot. Of course, he was not driving, but something in his life obstructed his ability to see accurately.

Balaam definitely doesn't rank in the top ten when it comes to Old Testament prophets, yet he holds a place in scripture as an example to us of how we should avoid certain barriers or blind spots to proper discernment; a principle that can aid us in our calling.

Numbers 22 tells us the story of a Moabite king named Balak who was afraid of his new neighbors—the children of Israel. He heard the news about how Israel defeated other nations and was afraid that they were too powerful for him. So Balak sent for the prophet Balaam to curse the children of Israel to his advantage.

The story continues where Balak sent elders to convince the prophet to do what the king wanted done. When Balaam met the entourage of elders and heard about Balak's request, he went to God for direction. The Lord told Balaam, no, he was not allowed to curse those whom God had blessed. So Balaam refused to go to Balak.

Not willing to accept no for an answer, Balak sent more officials and this time promised Balaam money and prestige, but the prophet refused again. However, it was at this point that Balaam went back to God and asked God a second time, perhaps hoping that God would change His mind.

Later that evening, God said to Balaam, If the men come to call you, rise up and go with them, but still only what I tell you may you do" (verse 20). So the next day, Balaam packed his bags, and got on his donkey to go meet Balak. Consequently, God was angry and sent an angel to judge him. As Balaam was on his way to see Balak, the angel appeared in the middle of the road with a sword drawn ready to strike him with a fatal blow. Fortunately, even though Balaam could not see the angel, God opened the donkey's eyes to see the angel.

On three separate occasions, the donkey tried to avoid the angel by going a different way. But each time, Balaam reacted in anger and struck the donkey. Finally, God opened the donkey's mouth, and it cried out to Balaam, "Why are you beating me ... haven't I been faithful to you, have I ever reacted like this before?" (paraphrased). Then God opened Balaam's eyes to see the angel ready to take him out! Balaam fell flat on his face in repentance.

I believe what angered God so much was Balaam's persistence to go to Balak. His insistence revealed a heart issue. He understood God's responses of no, but after Balak offered him money and power, Balaam told the messengers to wait around while he checked in with God again over the matter. His continued effort to satisfy Balak was a direct result of pride and greed, which was sin against God. It fueled his act of disobedience. Consequently, his sin formed a blind spot.

This sin blinded the prophet in two ways. First, it blinded him from properly discerning God's Will. Balaam was more focused on the reward than pleasing God (see Jude 11). Secondly, the sin blinded him from seeing the angel standing in his way. In other words, it was pride and greed that blinded Balaam to the fact that it was God who didn't agree with Him. Balaam was making major decisions based on his own blindness.

What's interesting is that it was God opposing Balaam, not the devil. Balaam didn't understand God's boundaries. The price of disobedience could have cost him his life. But God had mercy on him by not killing him.

Sometimes we don't realize that we have blind spots. Sin can obstruct our view. Are there things in your heart that could be blinding you from discerning what God is really saying or showing you? Sometimes it's our obstinacy that blinds us. Sometimes it's resentment or unforgiveness. Whatever it may be, it could be blinding us from seeing God's viewpoint.

Author, Gordon Smith, reminds us of how the subtle temptations noted in Luke 4:1–13 can negatively influence our motives related to our callings. The desire for power, greed, material security, fame, and prestige can literally shipwreck our lives. He conveys further that "only when we are honest about our motives do we begin to discern our vocations well."[5]

If we have to pry the window of opportunity open, then perhaps it's not God's timing and/or it's not God's will. To push beyond what God originally intended can result in costly mistakes. Author, Laurie Beth Jones, summed it up by saying, "If you do everything you possibly can to get something to happen, and it doesn't, then an angel must be on the road somewhere, so don't beat the donkey ... look for the angel standing in the road."[6]

Discerning Well

At times, it may be difficult to accurately discern what God is saying. Sometimes getting the proper discernment may take the discipline of fasting and prayer to break the influence of our flesh and position us to hear God clearly. It may require repentance of something in our lives that we haven't acknowledged. Psalm 15 emphasizes that the one who can abide in God's tabernacle is the one who has clean hands and a pure heart. We must refuse to allow sin to affect our discernment.

We can develop good discernment because God gave each of us the faculties to recognize spiritual things. God will commune with us through our spirit, which has the capacity to receive insight, wisdom, instructions, and directions (see Proverbs 20:27). Those who don't know God cannot comprehend His way of doing things; it appears foolish to them. But for the Christian, following God's way is the right way; it's the only way.

Secondly, the Word of God teaches us how to discern prudently. The Psalmist said in Psalm 119:30, "I have chosen the way of truth; I have set my heart on your laws."[7] He further declared in verse 11, "I have thought much about your words and stored them in my heart so that they hold me back from sin."[8] To discern wisely requires a commitment to the Word of God. Dean Ron Deberry of Bethel College asserts:

> I've become convinced in my life that in order for a person to really fulfill the destiny and call God has on their life they have to exercise proper discernment and that discernment is best arrived at or developed through devotional study of God's word ... it's almost proportional to the amount of time they spend in God's word. Not academically ... but devotionally studying the word.[9]

God's Word is a treasure of knowledge and understanding, because wisdom begins with Him. Proverbs 4:11 describes God's Word as comprehensive insight in the ways and purposes of God.[10] The Word gives us insight into God's way of thinking. In the face of any circumstance, we can open the scriptures and ask God for wisdom concerning any matter.

Devotional time with God enhances our ability to discern God's heart. That time with Him sensitizes our spirit toward Him. Jesus spent time with God, and as a result, He knew God's heart and God's thoughts. The decisions

PROPER DISCERNMENT

He made were based on knowing His Father. The more we spend time with God, the more we take on His heart. It will help us make decisions on what would please Him.

Thirdly, the Holy Spirit will help us to discern and know the things God wants for us. First Corinthians 2:12 states, "Now we have received, not the spirit of the world, but the Spirit who is from God, that we might know the things that have been freely given to us by God."[11] And included in the things God wants us to know are His will, His timing, any opportunities, any restrictions, our season, our calling, and our gifts.

God equipped each of us to accomplish great things, more than we would have ever imagined. And like the tribe of Issachar, God wants us to discern what to do and when to do it.

If you ever find yourself struggling with a decision, I want to encourage you to use the prayer below. Even if you rephrase it in your own words, the key is to acknowledge God. He promised to direct your life and to grant you the wisdom to discern well so you can continue to make the right decisions on your journey to fulfilling your call.

Prayer

Lord, help me to recognize Your will and distinguish Your timing. Help me identify this season in my life so I know what I should do. Help me to discriminate and separate thoroughly in my heart and mind, Your opportunities, as well as, a closed door. Help me to always consider the question, "What is Your wisdom concerning this matter?" Give me the strength to accept your truth and choose Your way, and give me the confidence to know that the outcome of any situation will always be for my benefit and for Your glory. Thank You, Lord. I trust You with all my heart as I pursue Your call on my life. In Jesus' name, Amen.

Chapter 14

7 Principles

1. Godly discernment will enable you to know the difference between what's OK for you compared to God's best for you.

2. There was one group of people that had an unusual skill, the tribe of Issachar. Their skill was not described in terms of the ability to handle a spear or sword, but rather, they had the ability to discern the times and to know what Israel should do.

3. God determines a flight plan for each of us. Based on where God is taking us, He lays out the "call" itinerary. He determines the scope of what we're called to do. He determines the destination, and even the resources and provisions are preset.

4. If we discern God's time correctly, even in difficulty, then like Joseph, we can continue to be productive when we are in our calling.

5. Sometimes we don't realize that we have blind spots. Sin can obstruct our view. Are there things in your heart that could be blinding you from discerning what God is really saying or showing you?

6. If we have to pry the window of opportunity open, then perhaps, it's not God's timing and/or it's not God's will, and to push beyond what God originally intended can result in costly mistakes.

7. The more we spend time with God, the more we take on His heart. It will help us make decisions about what would please Him.

APPENDIX 1

Books

1. *Now, Discover Your Strengths,* by Marcus Buckingham & Donald O. Clifton.
2. *Discover Your God-Given Gifts,* by Don and Katie Fortune.
3. *Live Your Calling,* by Kevin & Kay Marie Brennfleck.
4. *S.H.A.P.E.,* by Erik Rees.
5. *Spiritual Gifts – Their purpose and Power,* by Bryan Carraway.
6. *Discover Your Spiritual Gifts,* by C. Peter Wagner.
7. *What You Do Best in the Body of Christ,* by Bruce Bugbee.

ENDNOTES

Chapter 1
1. Lucado, Max. *You Are Special: The Animated Story.* Directed by Andrea Jobe. Produced by Tom Newman and David Pitts. 2000.
2. ibid.
3. "Call." Merriam-Webster.com. Merriam-Webster, 2009. 5 March 2009.
4. Warren, Rick. *The Purpose Driven Life.* Zondervan, 2002.
5. Nasa.gov. *Hubble Space Telescope.* http://www.nasa.gov/mission_pages/hubble/science/cosmic-expansion.html (accessed April 30, 2012).
6. Psalms 33:6 (NLT).
7. Hebrews 1:3 (NLT).
8. Genesis 1:11 (NIV).
9. Romans 8:28 (HCSB).
10. Isaiah 46:10 (CJB).
11. "Echo." Merriam-Webster.com. Merriam-Webster, 2009. 5 March 2009.

Chapter 2

1. Maxwell, John C. *How Successful People Think.* New York: Center Street, 2009.
2. Munroe, Dr. Myles. *Understanding The Power and Purpose of Men.* Whitaker House, 2001.
3. Colossians 1:16–17 PP13, from Adam Clarke Commentary, PC Study Bible Copyright 1993–1998 Bible Soft.
4. Genesis 1:26 (NKJV)
5. Isaiah 49:15 (DOUAY-RHEIMS)
6. John 3:16 (NKJV)
7. Daniel 12:3 (HCSB)
8. "Glorify" (from *Vine's Expository Dictionary of Biblical Words*)(Copyright (C) 1985, Thomas Nelson Publishers).
9. "Copiousness." Merriam-Webster.com. Merriam-Webster, 2009. 3 March 2009.
10. "Represent." Merriam-Webster.com. Merriam-Webster, 2009. 3 March 2009.

Chapter 3

1. MacDonald, Gordon. "Leader's Insight: When Leaders Implode." *christianitytoday.com.* November 6, 2006. http://www.christianitytoday.com/le/2006/november-online-only/cln61106.html (accessed December 19, 2010).
2. White, James Emery. "Leadership – Survival Skills." *ChristianityToday.com.* July 27, 2009. http://www.christianitytoday.com/le/2009/summer/survivalskills.html (accessed December 19, 2010).
3. wikipedia.org. "Ben_Johnson_(sprinter)." *wikipedia.org.* http://en.wikipedia.org/wiki/Ben_Johnson_(sprinter) (accessed April 5, 2011).
4. Harrell, Keith. *Attitude is Everything: 10 Life Changing Steps to Turning Attitude into Action.* New York: Harper Collins Publishers, Inc., 2000, 2003.Df

5. Cashman, Kevin. *Leadership from the Inside Out: Becoming a Leader for Life.* San Francisco: Berrett-Koehler Publishers, Inc., 2008.
6. Graves, Stephen, Thomas Addington, and Sean Womack. *Connerstones For Calling.* Word Publishing, 2000.
7. Internet World Stats. *Internet Usage Statistics – The Internet Big Picture.* December 31, 2011. http://www.internetworldstats.com/stats.htm (accessed August 5, 2012).
8. "Usain Bolt." *wikipedia.org.* http://en.wikipedia.org/wiki/Usain_Bolt (accessed April 5, 2011).Ddfd
9. Worldometers.info. *Worldometers – World Statistics Updated in Real Time.* http://www.worldometers.info/computers/ (accessed April 5, 2011).
10. Alden, Andrew. "Six Things to Know About the Earth's Mantle." *About.com, Geology.* http://geology.about.com/od/mantle/tp/mantleintro.htm (accessed April 6, 2011).
11. History, American Museum of Natural. "The Nature of Diamonds." *Diamonds – American Museum of Natural History.* http://www.amnh.org/exhibitions/diamonds/carbon.html (accessed April 9, 2011).Dfdf
12. Romans 8:18–19 (NKJV).

Chapter 4

1. Meyer, Allan, and Helen Meyer. *Search For Life.* Careforce Lifekeys, 2006.
2. Ephesians 1:16–17 (TLB).
3. *Vine's Expository Dictionary of Biblical Words.* Thomas Nelson Publishers, 1985.
4. 2 Corinthians 5:17 (NLT).
5. New Unger's Bible Dictionary. *Image of God.* PC Study Bible, 1993–1998.
6. Colossians 3:10 (TLB).

7. Hughes, Selwyn. "To Look at You." In *Everyday with Jesus Bible*, by Holman Christian Standard Bible, 102. Nashville: Holman Bible Publishers, 2004.

Chapter 5

1. John 5:19 (ESV).
2. Mark 1:35 (NIV).
3. John 4:34 (ASV).
4. John 15:10 (TLB).
5. Hughes, Selwyn. "The Cross's Magnetism." In *Everyday with Jesus Bible*, by Holman Christian Standard Bible, 651. Nashville: Holman Bible Publishers, 2004.
6. 1 John 3:17 (NAS).
7. 1 John 3:22 (NLT).

Chapter 6

1. *Dream Center.* http://dreamcenter.org/ (accessed 6 1, 2011).
2. Barna, George, and Matthew Barnett. *The Cause Within You.* Austin: Barna Books, 2011, 10.
3. Barna and Barnett, 11.
4. Barna and Barnett, 13.
5. Wuest, Kenneth S. *The New Testament: An Expanded Translation.* Williams B. Eerdmans Publishing Company, 1961.
6. ibid.
7. Barna, George, and Matthew Barnett. *The Cause Within You.* Austin: Barna Books, 2011, 3-7.
8. Philippians 3:7 (NKJV).
9. Phil 3:7 (TLB).
10. Phil 3:13 (TLB).
11. Phil 3:8 (KJV).

ENDNOTES

Chapter 7

1. Romans 1:1 (NIV).
2. *The American Heritage College Dictionary 3rd Addition.* Houghton Mifflin Company, 2000.
3. Wuest, Kenneth S. *The New Testament: An Expanded Translation.* Williams B Eerdmans Publishing Company, 1961.
4. Graves, Stephen, Thomas Addington, and Sean Womack. *Connerstones For Calling.* Word Publishing, 2000.
5. Munroe, Myles. *In Pursuit of Purpose.* Destiny Image Publishers, Inc., 1992.
6. Murdock, Dr. Mike. *Jesus was a Double Diamond.* Wisdom International Inc., 1990.
7. Psalm 69:9 (TLB).
8. Warren, Rick. *The Purpose Driven Life.* Zondervan, 2002.
9. DeBerry, Dr. Ron, interview by Kelvin Collins. *Academic Dean, Bethel College* (12 30, 2010).
10. Smith, Gordon T. *Courage & Calling.* InterVarsity Press, 1999.
11. Brennfleck, Kevin, and Kay Marie Brennfleck. *Live Your Calling.* San Francisco: Jossey-Bass, 2005.
12. Guinness, Os. *The Call: Finding and Fulfilling the Central Purpose of Your Life.* W. Publishing Group, 1998, 2003.
13. MacDonald, Gordon. *Ordering Your Private World.* Thomas Nelson Publishers, 1984, 1985, 2003.
14. Guinness, Os. *The Call: Finding and Fulfilling the Central Purpose of Your Life.* W. Publishing Group, 1998, 2003.
15. Nelson's Illustrated Bible Dictionary, Copyright © 1986, Thomas Nelson Publishers.
16. Barnett, Matthew. *The Cause Within You.* Tyndale House Publishers, Inc., 2011.
17. Trickett, David, interview by Kelvin Collins. President of Iliff School of Theology (12 28, 2010).

18. Glenn, Reynolds, interview by Kelvin Collins. *Senior Pastor, Bethel Church, Hampton VA* (March 22, 2011).
19. 1 Corinthians 12:18 (NKJV).
20. CBS.com. *Undercover Boss.* http://www.cbs.com/primetime/undercover_boss/video/?pid=4DY_HKu1MxY7mkWjKHSFZgqajQL_SNv6 (accessed October 20, 2011).
21. 1 Corinthians 12:22 (TLB).
22. Tonsils Homoepathy, Heath & Medical. *Homoeopathy Ensures Healthy Safety.* http://www.ovihams.com/tonsillitis/about.htm (accessed June 3, 2012).
23. Ecclesiastes 11:4 (NLT).

Chapter 8

1. 2 Samuel 18:29 (NIV).
2. Numbers 18:7 (TLB).
3. Munroe, Dr. Myles. *The Principles and Power of Vision.* New Kensington, PA: Whitaker House, 2003.
4. 2 Samuel 18:22 (BBE).
5. Jamieson, Fausset, and Brown Commentary. *2 Samuel 18:23.* PC Study Bible, 1993–1998.
6. Maxwell, John. *The 21 Most Powerful Minutes in a Leader's Day.* Nashville: Thomas Nelson, Inc., 2000.

Chapter 9

1. "Personality." Merriam-Webster.com. Merriam-Webster, 2012. 2 December 2012.
2. Rees, Erik. *S.H.A.P.E. Finding & Fufilling Your Unique Purpose for Life.* Grand Rapids: Zondervan, 2006.
3. Wagner, C. Peter. *Discovering Your Spiritual Gifts.* Ventura: Regal Books, 2002–2005.
4. Carraway, Bryan. *Spiritual Gifts.* Enumclaw, WA: Pleasant Word, 2005.

ENDNOTES

5. Kinghorn, Kenneth Cain. *Discovering Your Spiritual Gifts: A Personal Inventory Method*. Grand Rapids: Zondervan, 1981.
6. Fortune, Don, and Katie Fortune. *Discover Your God-Given Gifts*. Grand Rapids: Chosen Books, 1987.
7. Warren, Rick. *The Purpose Driven Church*. Grand Rapids: Zondervan, 1995.
8. 2 Kings 4:4 (NKJV).
9. Wikipedia.org. http://en.wikipedia.org/wiki/Lyrebird (accessed 4 18, 2012).
10. Proverbs 14:23 (HCSB).
11. Nelson's Illustrated Dictionary Bible. *Grace*. Prod. BibleSoft PC Study Bible. Thomas Nelson Publishers, 1986.
12. 1 Corinthians 15:9–10 (TLB).
13. 1 Corinthians 15:10 (TLB).
14. Psalm 116:12 (KJV).
15. James 4:6 (RSV).
16. Murray, Andrew. *Humility*. New Kingsington: Whitaker House, 1982, 16-17.
17. Murray, 19.

Chapter 10

1. Stewardship. ILLUSTRATIONS OF BIBLE TRUTHS. Copyright © 1995, 1998 by AMG International, Inc. Electronic Database. Copyright © 1997, 2003, 2005, 2006 by Biblesoft, Inc.
2. THE BIBLE EXPOSITION COMMENTARY: NEW TESTAMENT Copyright © 1989 by Chariot Victor Publishing, and imprint of Cook Communication Ministries.
3. Buckingham, Marcus, and Donald O Clifton. *Now, Discover Your Strengths*. New York: The Free Press, 2001.
4. Barna, George. "The Barna Group – Awareness of Spiritual Gifts is Changing." *The Barna Group – Awareness of*

Spiritual Gifts is Changing. The Barna Group. (accessed 7 22, 2012).
5. Munroe, Dr. Myles. *Daily Power and Prayer 365 Day Devotional.* New Kensington, PA: Whitaker House, 2007
6. Rees, Erik. *S.H.A.P.E. Finding & Fulfilling Your Unique Purpose for Life.* Grand Rapids: Zondervan, 2006.
7. Munroe, Dr. Myles. *The Principles and Power of Vision.* New Kensington, PA: Whitaker House, 2003.
8. Nelson's Illustrated Bible Dictionary. *TRADE AND TRAVEL.* Prod. Thomas Nelson Publishers. 1986. Electronic Database. Copyright © 1997, 2003, 2005, 2006 by Biblesoft, Inc.
9. Matthew 25:14. JAMIESON, FAUSSET AND BROWN COMMENTARY, Electronic Database. Copyright © 1997, 2003, 2005, 2006 by Biblesoft, Inc.
10. Matthew 25:15. CLARKE's COMMENTARY, Electronic Database. Copyright © 1996, 2003, 2005 by Biblesoft, Inc.
11. James 1:5 (KJV).
12. 2 Corinthians 9:8 (AMP).
13. Matthew 7:7 (NIV).
14. Munroe, Dr. Myles. *Daily Power and Prayer 365 Day Devotional.* New Kensington, PA: Whitaker House, 2007.
15. Matthew 5:16 (HCSB).
16. Romans 12:1 (CJB).
17. Rees, Erik. *S.H.A.P.E. Finding & Fulfilling Your Unique Purpose for Life.* Grand Rapids: Zondervan, 2006.
18. Luke 19:13; JAMIESON, FAUSSET AND BROWN COMMENTARY, Electronic Database. Copyright © 1997, 2003, 2005, 2006 by Biblesoft, Inc.
19. Luke 16:10 (NLT).
20. Warren, Rick. *The Purpose Driven Church.* Grand Rapids: Zondervan, 1995.
21. Matthew 25:21 (NLT).

Chapter 11

1. MacDonald, Gordon. *Ordering Your Private World.* Nashville: Thomas Nelson Publishers, 1984, 1985, 2003, 35.
2. MacDonald, 40.
3. Jones, Laura Beth. *Jesus CEO: Using Ancient Wisdom for Visionary Leadership.* New York: Hyperion, 1995.
4. 1 Peter 1:8 (TLB).
5. NFL.Com. *NFL Videos: Tebow Joins the set.* 11 18, 2011. http://www.nfl.com/videos/nfl-thursday-night-football/09000d5d8243b704/tebow-joins-the-set (accessed 11 22, 2011).
6. MacDonald, Gordon. *Ordering Your Private World.* Nashville: Thomas Nelson Publishers, 1984, 1985, 2003.
7. Jones, Laura Beth. *Jesus CEO: Using Ancient Wisdom for Visionary Leadership.* New York: Hyperion, 1995.
8. *Winchester Mystery House.* 11 22, 2011. http://www.winchestermysteryhouse.com/.
9. http://en.wikipedia.org/wiki/Winchester_Mystery_House (accessed 11 22, 2011).
10. I Corinthians 3:14 (Moffat translation).
11. *Walt Disney.* http://en.wikipedia.org/wiki/Walt_Disney (accessed 11 7, 2011).
12. ibid.
13. "History of Oral Roberts University." www.dingman.com/oru_history.pdf (accessed 2 15, 2012).
14. Harrell, Jr., David Edwin. *Oral Roberts: An American Life.* Bloomington: Indiana University Press, 1985.
15. Luke 11:2 (KJV).
16. "History of Oral Roberts University." www.dingman.com/oru_history.pdf (accessed 2 15, 2012).
17. Jakes, T.D. *Maximize the Moment; God's Action Plan for Your Life.* New York: Berkley Publishing Group, 1999.

Chapter 12

1. Thinkexist.com*Lewis Carroll Quotes*http://www.thinkexist.com/quotation
2. James 1:5 (TLB).
3. Psalm 119:105 (NLT).
4. Psalm 119:133 (NIV).
5. Joshua 1:8 (NIV).
6. Proverbs 4:26 (HCSB).
7. *Yosemite National Park Nature and Science*http://www.nps.gov/yose/naturescience/index.htm
8. *Friends of YOSAR Yosemites Search and Rescue*http://www.friendsofyosar.org/about_us/aboutYOSAR.html
9. *What is a compass used for?*http://www.trails.com/about_3646_what-compass-used.html
10. http://www.merriam-webster.com/dictionary/peace
11. *MLB.com*http://mlb.mlb.com/mlb/official_info/umpires/rules_interest.jsp#9.00
12. Colossians 3:15 (NKJV).
13. *The Power of The Call,* Broadman & Holman Publishers 1997.
14. Crystal Lewis. "Trust Me." *Fearless* 2000.
15. Isaiah 12:2 (KJV).

Chapter 13

1. "US Airways Flight 1549." *wikipedia.org*. Http://en.wikipedia.org/wiki/US_Airways_Flight_1549 (accessed 7 19, 2011).
2. "A & S Interview: Sully's Tale." *www.airspcemag.com*. Air and Space Magazine. http://www.airspcemag.com/flight-today/Sullys-Tale.html (accessed 9 2, 2011).
3. "US Airways Flight 1549." *wikipedia.org*. Http://en.wikipedia.org/wiki/US_Airways_Flight_1549 (accessed 7 19, 2011).

ENDNOTES

4. ibid.
5. Ecclesiastes 3:1 (NKJV).
6. Genesis 16:2 (NKJV).
7. Genesis 18:14 (ASV).
8. Folz, Dr. Howard L., and Ruth Ford. *For Such a Time As This: Strategic Missions Power Shifts for the 21st Century.* William Carey Library, 2000.
9. Maxwell, John. *The 21 Most Powerful Minutes in a Leader's Day.* Nashville: Thomas Nelson, Inc., 2000.
10. John 9:4 (TLB).
11. "US Airways Flight 1549." *wikipedia.org.* Http://en.wikipedia.org/wiki/US_Airways_Flight_1549 (accessed 7 19, 2011).
12. ibid.
13. "A & S Interview: Sully's Tale." *www.airspcemag.com.* Air and Space Magazine. http://www.airspcemag.com/flight-today/Sullys-Tale.html (accessed 9 2, 2011).
14. Murdock, Mike. *Jesus was a Double Diamond.* Dallas: Wisdom International Inc., 1990.
15. "Decoding the Skies." *nationalgeographic.com.* National Geographic. http://channel.nationalgeographic.com/series/known-universe/4502/Overview#tab-facts#ixzz1MMEPGH7m (accessed 1 3, 2012).
16. Isaiah 43:19 (NIV).
17. Isaiah 55:10 (NIV).
18. Galatians 6:9 (NLT).
19. Psalm 30:5 (NKJV).
20. Britannica Online Encyclopedia. http://www.britannica.com/EBchecked/topic/64553/winter (accessed 4 1, 2012).
21. Jakes, T.D. *Maximize the Moment; God's Action Plan for Your Life.* New York: Berkley Publishing Group, 1999.
22. Ecclesiastes 3:14 (NLT).
23. Ephesians 3:20 (TLB).

Chapter 14

1. Stanley, Dr. Charles. *The Power of a Discerning Spirit.* 9 25, 2011. http://www.intouch.org/you/life-principles-notes (accessed 12 1, 2011).
2. Psalm 105:17 (TLB).
3. Genesis 40:14 (NKJV).
4. Jakes, T.D. *Maximize the Moment; God's Action Plan for Your Life.* New York: Berkley Publishing Group, 1999.
5. Smith, Gordon T. *Courage & Calling.* InterVarsity Press, 1999.
6. Jones, Laura Beth. *Jesus CEO: Using Ancient Wisdom for Visionary Leadership.* New York: Hyperion, 1995.
7. Psalm 119:30 (NIV).
8. Psalm 119:11 (TLB).
9. DeBerry, Dr. Ron, interview by Kelvin Collins. *Academic Dean, Bethel College* (12 30, 2010).
10. Proverbs 4:11 (AMP).
11. 1 Corinthians 2:12 (NKJV).

ABOUT THE AUTHOR

Kelvin is the founder of PsalmsArt Ministry, a ministry that shares biblical principles through teaching, music and creative arts and community outreaches. He is an ordained minister and has served in leadership roles in the body of Christ for over the last 25 years. His passion is to aid others in discovering their purpose and calling in life. He is a writer, teacher, playwright and musician. Kelvin and his wife, Angela and their children are currently serving in their local church in the Virginia Hampton Roads area.

For more information go to www.Psalmsart.org

www.ingramcontent.com/pod-product-compliance
Lightning Source LLC
Chambersburg PA
CBHW020400080526
44584CB00014B/1110